WONDER

April 26, 1987

Dear Kevin,

I give you this little devotional book for your Baptism so that as you identify your life with Jesus, you also obey His command:

"... grow in the grace and knowledge of our Lord and Saviour, Jesus Christ. To Him be glory both now and forever." II Peter 3:18

Love,
Mom

Tyndale House Publishers, Inc.

DER

What a kid should know

Selections from *The Living Bible* compiled by Edythe Draper

Wheaton, Illinois

WONDER
All Scripture passages are from *The Living Bible,* paraphrased by Kenneth
N. Taylor, © 1971 by Tyndale House Publishers.

Second printing, May 1986. Library of Congress Catalog Card Number
84-51059. ISBN 0-8423-8385-9. © 1984 by Edythe Draper. All rights reserved.
Printed in the United States of America.

SING·TO·THE·LORD,

FOR·HE·HAS·DONE·

WONDERFUL·THINGS·

ISAIAH 12:5

The earth is filled with God's tender love.

God's marvelous love is so great that you will never see the end of it or fully know or understand it.

God prepares the earth for his people and sends them rich harvests of grain. The pastures are filled with flocks of sheep, and the valleys are carpeted with grain.

All the world shouts with joy and sings.

PSALM 33:5   EPHESIANS 3:17, 18, 19
PSALM 65:9, 12, 13

Chelsea Kellow, age 9

Raechel Anderson, age 6

Be glad for all
God is planning for you.

You have a wonderful future ahead
of you.

No man has even seen, heard or
even imagined what wonderful
things God has ready for those who
love the Lord.

Be delighted with the Lord.
Then he will give you all your
heart's desires.

ROMANS 12:12   PROVERBS 23:18
1 CORINTHIANS 2:9   PSALM 37:4

Clap for joy!

For the Lord is beyond words. He is the great King of all the earth.

Sing out your praises to our God, our King. Yes, sing your highest praises to our King, the King of all the earth.

How great is the Lord!
How much we should praise him!

PSALM 47:1, 2, 6, 7   PSALM 48:1

4

The Lord is God!

He made us. We are his people, the sheep of his pasture.

We, your people, will thank you forever and forever, praising your greatness.

Come, kneel before the Lord our Maker, for he is our God. Hear him calling you today and come to him.

PSALM 100:3
PSALM 79:13
PSALM 95:6, 7

Ami Sparkman, age 7

The Lord watches over all the plans and paths of godly men.

For God loved the world so much that he gave his only Son so that anyone who believes in him shall not die but have eternal life.

Not one sparrow can fall to the ground without your Father knowing it. You are more valuable to him than many sparrows.

PSALM 1:6   JOHN 3:16   MATTHEW 10:29, 31

JANUARY

6

O Lord, you are so good and kind.

How precious it is, Lord, to realize that you are thinking about me constantly. I can't even count how many times a day your thoughts turn toward me. And when I waken in the morning, you are still thinking of me!

Your goodness and unfailing kindness shall be with me all of my life.

PSALM 86:5   PSALM 139:17, 18   PSALM 23:6

You are my God.

You know everything about me. You know when I sit or stand. You know my every thought. You made all the delicate, inner parts of my body. You saw me before I was born and planned each day of my life before I began to breathe. Every day was recorded in your book.

ISAIAH 25:1   PSALM 139:1, 2, 13, 16

What does the Lord your God require of you?

1. To listen carefully to all he says to you.
2. To obey for your own good the commandments.
3. To love him and to worship him with all your heart and soul.

DEUTERONOMY 10:12, 13

Steve Schick, age 9

Loving God means doing what he tells you to do.

He has told you what he wants, and this is all it is: to be fair and just and merciful, and to walk humbly with your God.

Learn as you go along what pleases the Lord. Please him always in everything.

1 JOHN 5:3   MICAH 6:8   EPHESIANS 5:10
2 CORINTHIANS 5:9

To do right honors God.

I would have you learn this great fact: that a life of doing right is the wisest life there is.

Have two goals: wisdom—that is, knowing and doing right—and common sense. They will keep you safe from defeat and disaster.

PROVERBS 14:2   PROVERBS 4:11
PROVERBS 3:21, 23

Just tell me what to do and I will do it, Lord.

Lord, don't let me make a mess of things. If you will only help me to want your will, then I will follow your laws even more closely.

Give me common sense to apply your rules to everything I do.

PSALM 119:33, 31, 32, 125

**God gave you his rules
so you would know
what he wanted you to do.**

1 Tell the truth.

2 Be fair.

3 Live at peace with everyone.

4 Don't plot harm to others.

5 Don't say that something is true
when it isn't.

ROMANS 9:4 ZECHARIAH 8:16

Katy Botts, age 8

Live one day at a time.

Let God have all your
worries and cares. He is
always thinking about you
and watching everything
that concerns you.

Commit everything you do to the
Lord. Trust him to help you do it
and he will.

MATTHEW 6:34   1 PETER 5:7   PSALM 37:5

When you were a small child you were taught the holy Scriptures.

You know they are true for you know that you can trust those of us who have taught you.

The whole Bible is useful to teach us what is true and to make us realize what is wrong in our lives. It straightens us out and helps us do what is right.

2 TIMOTHY 3:15, 14, 16

Todd Hoskins, age 9

All God's words are right.

They protect us.
They make us wise.
They keep us away from harm.
They give success to those who
  obey them.
God's laws are perfect.

PSALM 19:7, 8, 11, 7

**Your name is known
all over the earth,
O God.**

Mitchell Freeman, age 8

You are praised everywhere.

How wonderful are your deeds,
O God. How great your power!

You constantly satisfy the
hunger and thirst of every living
thing. Your marvelous deeds shall
be on every tongue.

O Lord, there is no one else like
you.

PSALM 48:10   PSALM 66:3   PSALM 145:16, 6
JEREMIAH 10:6

His great love for us.

God showed his great love for us by
sending Christ to die for us while
we were still sinners.

If we confess our sins to him, he
can be depended on to forgive us
and to cleanse us from every
wrong.

ROMANS 5:8   1 JOHN 1:9

Salvation comes from our God.

You alone have the words that give eternal life. You are the holy Son of God.

I confess my sins. I am sorry for what I have done. And you forgive me. All my guilt is gone.

REVELATON 7:10
JOHN 6:69
PSALM 38:18
PSALM 32:5

Christopher Andreoli, age 7

Every promise from God shall surely come true.

It is impossible for God to tell a lie.

He isn't one to say "yes" when he means "no." He always does exactly what he says.

God doesn't change his mind like humans do. He never forgets his promises.

LUKE 1:37   2 CORINTHIANS 1:19   PSALM 111:5

All living things shall thank you, Lord.

You give them their food as they need it. You constantly satisfy the hunger and thirst of every living thing.

You are concerned for men and animals alike. O Lord, the earth is full of your lovingkindness.

I will thank you by living as I should.

PSALM 145:10, 15, 16   PSALM 36:6
PSALM 119:64, 7

Honor your father and mother.

God has put them in authority over you.

This is the first of God's Ten Commandments that ends with a promise. And this is the promise: that if you honor your father and mother, yours will be a long life, full of happiness.

EXODUS 20:12   EPHESIANS 6:1, 2, 3

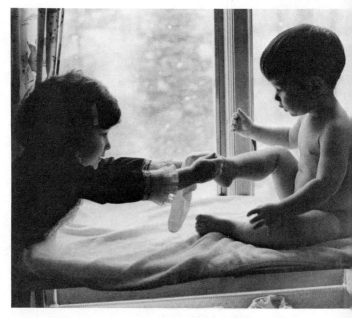

Don't let anyone think little of you because you are young.

Be a pattern for them. Keep a close watch on all you do and think. Stay true to what is right and God will reward you and use you to help others.

1 TIMOTHY 4:12, 16

Harsh words cause quarrels.

Don't get involved in foolish arguments, which only upset people and make them angry. Don't quarrel with anyone. Be at peace with everyone, just as much as possible.

Conquer evil by doing good.

PROVERBS 15:1   2 TIMOTHY 2:23
ROMANS 12:18, 21

Don't think only of yourself.

Try to think of the other person, and what is best for him. You must love and help your neighbors.

Don't repay evil for evil. Don't snap back at those who say unkind things about you. Instead, pray for God's help for them. For we are to be kind to others.

1 CORINTHIANS 10:24   JAMES 2:8   1 PETER 3:9

I think you can.
I know you can.

The laws of Jehovah.

Think about them every day and every night so that you will be sure to obey all of them. For only then will you succeed.

These laws are not just words. Those who obey them shall be great in the Kingdom of Heaven.

Lord, teach me your rules.

EXODUS 35:1   JOSHUA 1:8
DEUTERONOMY 32:47
MATTHEW 5:19   PSALM 119:12

God loves whatever is just and good.

The earth is filled with his tender love. Everything he does is worthy of our trust.

Let everyone in all the world— men, women and children— fear the Lord and stand in awe of him. For when he spoke the world began. It appeared at his command.

PSALM 33:4, 5, 8, 9

Amy Cook, age 8

O Lord God!
You have made
the heavens and earth.

The earth belongs to God.
Everything in all the world is his.
He is the one who pushed the
oceans back to let dry land appear.
He simply spoke and the heavens
were formed, and all the galaxies
of stars.

   Day and night alike belong to
him. He made the starlight and the
sun. He made the summer and
winter too.

JEREMIAH 32:17   PSALM 24:1
PSALM 33:6   PSALM 74:16

Whatever he wants to do, God does.

The sun won't rise, the stars won't shine, if he commands it so. He directs the snow, the showers, and storm to fall upon the earth.

Jesus stood up and motioned to the wind and waves, and the storm stopped and all was calm.

The Lord our God, the Almighty, reigns.

JOB 23:13   JOB 9:7   JOB 37:6
MATTHEW 8:26   REVELATION 19:6

Chris Imhoff, age 8

God alone has all power.

World events are under his control.
He removes kings and sets others
on their thrones. He gives wise men
their wisdom and teachers their
knowledge.

Riches and honor come from God
alone. His hand controls power and
might.

DANIEL 2:20, 21   1 CHRONICLES 20:12

Pray about everything.

God is listening when we talk to him. We can be sure that he will answer us.

God will listen to us whenever we ask him for anything in line with his will.

1 JOHN 5:15, 14

Whatever is good comes to us from God.

Food and drink . . . even this pleasure is from the hand of God. For who can eat or enjoy apart from him?

The Lord is good. When trouble comes, he is the place to go. And he knows everyone who trusts in him.

JAMES 1:17   ECCLESIASTES 2:24, 25   NAHUM 1:7

Cling tightly to your faith in Christ.

God will make you the kind of children he wants to have. He will make you as good as you wish you could be.

Your greatest joy will be that you belong to him. The tender kindness of our God and of the Lord Jesus Christ has made all this possible for you.

1 TIMOTHY 1:19   2 THESSALONIANS 1:11, 12

2

Jon Sanchez, age 8

Come to me with your ears wide open.

"I will tell you secrets you haven't heard. For I know the plans I have for you," says the Lord. "They are plans for good."

How very much our heavenly Father loves us, for he allows us to be called his children. And since we are his children, we will share his treasures.

ISAIAH 55:3   ISAIAH 48:6   JEREMIAH 29:11
1 JOHN 3:1   ROMANS 8:17

Lord,
you are good
and do only good.

Your goodness and unfailing kindness shall be with me all of my life. Afterwards I will live with you forever in your home.

Jesus died for us so that we can live with him forever.

How much God loves us!

PSALM 119:68   PSALM 23:6
1 THESSALONIANS 5:10   1 JOHN 4:16

God is on our side.

He tells us that he loves us dearly.

If God is on our side, who can ever be against us? Since he did not spare even his own Son for us but gave him up for us all, won't he also surely give us everything else?

ROMANS 8:31   1 JOHN 4:16   ROMANS 8:31, 32

Sing to the Lord with thankful hearts.

It is right to praise him. For all God's words are right, and everything he does is worthy of our trust.

Let the trees in the woods sing for joy before the Lord. Let the waves clap their hands in glee. Let everything alive give praises to the Lord.

You praise him!

COLOSSIANS 3:16   PSALM 33:1, 4
1 CHRONICLES 16:33   PSALM 98:8   PSALM 150:6

The good man does not escape all troubles— he has them too.

But the Lord helps him in each and every one.

Problems and trials help us learn to be patient. Let not your heart be troubled.

Put God to the test and see how kind he is! See for yourself the way his mercies shower down on all who trust him.

John Goodell, age 7

PSALM 34:19
PSALM 34:8
ROMANS 5:3
JOHN 14:1

FEBRUARY

7

The Lord will listen to me and answer when I call to him.

Day by day the Lord pours out his love upon me, and through the night I sing his songs and pray to God who gives me life.

The Lord has shown me that his never-failing love protects me like the walls of a fort.

PSALM 4:3   PSALM 42:8   PSALM 31:21

8

Emily Showalter, age 9

A life of doing right is the wisest life there is.

Carry out God's instructions. Don't forget them. For they will lead you to real living.

He has told you what he wants, and this is all it is: to be fair and just and merciful and to walk humbly with your God.

Keep these thoughts ever in mind.

PROVERBS 4:11, 13   MICAH 6:8   PROVERBS 4:21

Follow my instructions.

Don't always be trying to get out of doing your duty, even when it's unpleasant.

Tackle every task that comes along, and if you honor God you can expect his blessing.

Obey your parents. This is the right thing to do because God has placed them in authority over you.

PROVERBS 3:2   ECCLESIASTES 8:2, 3
ECCLESIASTES 7:18   EPHESIANS 6:1

Help me to choose obedience.

Keep me far from every wrong, for I have chosen to do right.

If you will only help me to want your will, then I will follow your laws even more closely.

May I never forget your words. You are good and do only good. Make me follow your lead.

PSALM 119:36, 29, 30, 32, 43, 68

I am as a little child who doesn't know his way around.

Give me an understanding mind so that I can know the difference between what is right and what is wrong.

The Lord was glad that Solomon had asked for wisdom.

To learn, you must want to be taught.

1 KINGS 2:7, 9, 10   PROVERBS 12:1

Don't always be wishing for what you don't have.

You long for what others have, and can't afford it, so you start a fight to take it away from them.

A dry crust eaten in peace is better than steak every day along with arguing and fighting.

LUKE 12:15   JAMES 4:2   PROVERBS 17:1

Don't quarrel with anyone.

Work happily together. Don't try to act big. Don't think you know it all.

Love each other with brotherly love and take delight in honoring each other.

Never forget to be truthful and kind.

ROMANS 12:18, 16, 10   PROVERBS 3:3

14

HONEY

Kind words are like honey— enjoyable and healthful.

Aimee Wheeler, age 10

Be kind to each other. Share each other's troubles and problems.

The person who tries to be good, loving, and kind finds life, righteousness, and honor.

The character of even a child can be known by the way he acts— whether what he does is pure and right.

PROVERBS 16:24   EPHESIANS 4:32
GALATIANS 6:2   PROVERBS 21:21
PROVERBS 20:11

Beth Kenney, age 8

This is your wonderful thought for the day:

Jehovah is God both in heaven and down here upon the earth. There is no God other than him.

Riches and honor come from him. He is the Ruler of all mankind. His hand controls power and might.

DEUTERONOMY 4:39   1 CHRONICLES 29:12

The earth is controlled by Jehovah.

He sends the snow. He calls for warmer weather. He makes the green grass grow.

The earth belongs to God!

EXODUS 9:29   PSALM 147:16, 18, 8   PSALM 24:1

Everything we have has come from God.

If you have good eyesight and good hearing, thank God who gave them to you.

He gives life and breath to everything. He has made many parts for our bodies and has put each part just where he wants it.

The soul of every living thing is in the hand of God.

1 CHRONICLES 29:14   PROVERBS 20:12
ACTS 17:25   1 CORINTHIANS 12:18
JOB 12:10

I made you and I will care for you.

You don't need to be afraid of the dark any more, nor fear the dangers of the day. For he orders his angels to protect you wherever you go.

He is like a father, tender and understanding to those who reverence him.

ISAIAH 46:3   PSALM 91:5, 11   PSALM 103:13

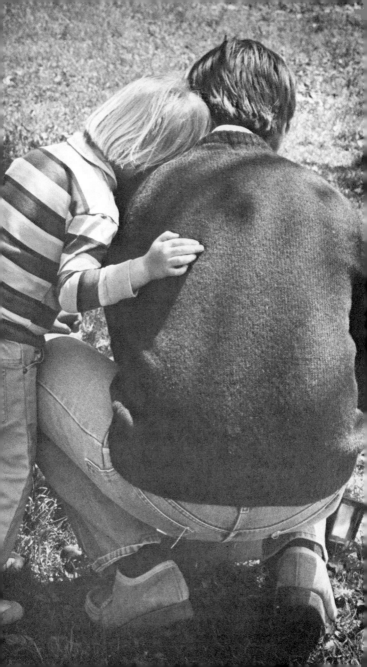

FEBRUARY

19

Love the Lord and follow his plan for your lives.

Loving God means doing what he tells us to do. And really, that isn't hard at all.

What does the Lord your God require of you? To listen carefully to all he says to you, to obey for your own good the commandments, and to love and worship him with all your heart and soul.

JOSHUA 22:5   1 JOHN 5:3
DEUTERONOMY 10:12, 13

He is for me!
How can I be afraid?

The Lord is on my side. He will help me. When trouble comes, he is the place to go. And he knows everyone who trusts in him.

He is good to everyone. He is always loving and kind.

PSALM 118:6, 7   NAHUM 1:7
PSALM 100:5   PSALM 145:9

Jeremy Botts, age 9

My God is changeless in his love for me.

Your love, O Lord, is as great as all the heavens. Your faithfulness reaches beyond the clouds.

Before the mountains were created, before the earth was formed, you are God without beginning or end. A thousand years are as yesterday to you! They are like a single hour!

PSALM 59:10   PSALM 36:5   PSALM 90:2, 4

God is a father to the fatherless.

How very much our heavenly Father loves us, for he allows us to be called his children.

His unchanging plan has always been to adopt us into his own family. That is why the Lord has said, "I will welcome you, and be a Father to you, and you will be my sons and daughters."

PSALM 68:5   1 JOHN 3:1   EPHESIANS 1:5
2 CORINTHIANS 6:17, 18

**Sons and daughters,
let me teach you
the importance of trusting
and fearing the Lord.**

Do you want a long, good life?
   Then watch your tongue. Keep
your lips from lying.
   Turn from all known sin and
spend your time in doing good.
   Try to live in peace with
everyone. Work hard at it.

PSALM 34:11, 12, 13, 14

Be patient with each other.

Allow for each other's faults. Love forgets mistakes. Nagging about them parts the best of friends.

Be gentle and ready to forgive. Never hold grudges. Remember, the Lord forgave you, so you must forgive others.

EPHESIANS 4:2   PROVERBS 17:9
COLOSSIANS 3:13

25

Why are you angry?

Now is the time to take off and throw away all these rotten clothes of anger, hatred, cursing, and dirty language.

Don't sin by nursing your grudge. Don't let the sun go down while you are still angry. Get over it quickly. For anger doesn't make us good, as God demands that we must be.

GENESIS 4:6   COLOSSIANS 3:8
EPHESIANS 4:26   JAMES 1:19

How often should I forgive?

Seven times?

"No," Jesus replied, "seventy times seven!"

Remember, the Lord forgave you, so you must forgive others.

If you love only those who love you, what good is that? If your enemy is hungry, give him food. If he is thirsty, give him something to drink.

MATTHEW 18:21, 22   PROVERBS 25:21
COLOSSIANS 3:13   MATTHEW 5:46

27

Don't forget to be kind.

Give to those who ask, and don't turn away from those who want to borrow. It is better to give than to receive.

Do good. Share what you have.

Whatever you do, do it with kindness and love. Love is never selfish.

HEBREWS 13:2   MATTHEW 5:42
ACTS 20:35   HEBREWS 13:16
1 CORINTHIANS 16:14   1 CORINTHIANS 13:5

Jennifer Miller, age 6

T HANK YOU
PLEASE
i LiKE YOU
YOU ARE NICE
LET ME H E LP YOU

The Lord delights in kind words.

Whenever we can we should always be kind to everyone. Be gentle and truly polite to all.

Kind words are like honey— enjoyable and healthful.

PROVERBS 15:26   GALATIANS 6:10
TITUS 3:2   PROVERBS 16:24

Let me describe for you a worthless and a wicked man.

First, he is a constant liar. He signals what he wants to his friends with eyes and feet and fingers.

Next, his heart is full of disobedience. And he spends his time thinking of all the evil he can do.

Stay away from evil men. Seek the Lord.

PROVERBS 6:12, 13, 14   PROVERBS 2:12
ISAIAH 51:1

All men are sinners.

No one is good. No one in all the world is innocent. No one has ever really followed God's paths. All have gone wrong. No one anywhere has kept on doing what is right. Yes, all have sinned.

Yet now God declares us "not guilty" if we trust in Jesus Christ.

ROMANS 3:10, 11, 12, 23, 24

God's great kindness.

Right now God is ready to welcome you. Today he is ready to save you.

For God loved the world so much that he gave his only Son so that anyone who believes in him shall not die but have eternal life.

2 CORINTHIANS 6:1, 2   JOHN 3:16

Jennifer Brown, age 6

Let everything alive give praises to the Lord!

Let the trees in the woods sing for joy before the Lord.

Praise him, sun and moon, and all you twinkling stars. Praise him, skies above. Let everything he has made give praise to him!

Come, everyone, and clap for joy!

PSALM 150:6   1 CHRONICLES 16:33
PSALM 148:3, 4, 5   PSALM 47:1

John Miller, age 8

Our God made the heavens!

Give him the glory he deserves! Bring your offering and come to worship him. For the Lord is great, and should be greatly praised.

Come before him with thankful hearts. Let us sing him psalms of praise. For the Lord is a great God!

PSALM 96:5, 8   1 CHRONICLES 16:25
PSALM 95:2, 3

MARCH

5

Bring your offering.

On every Lord's Day each of you should put aside something from what you have earned during the week. The amount depends on how much the Lord has helped you earn.

The godly person gives to the poor. His good deeds will be an honor to him forever.

PSALM 96:8   1 CORINTHIANS 16:2
2 CORINTHIANS 9:9

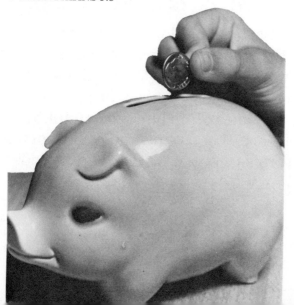

Happy is the person who feeds the poor.

If you really want to give, then it isn't important how much you have to give. God wants you to give what you have, not what you haven't.

Cheerful givers are the ones God prizes.

PROVERBS 22:9   2 CORINTHIANS 8:12
2 CORINTHIANS 9:7

Whatever you do, do well.

Let everyone be sure that he is doing his very best. Then he will have the personal satisfaction of work well done. He won't need to compare himself with someone else.

Tackle every task that comes along, and if you honor God you can expect his blessing.

ECCLESIASTES 9:10   GALATIANS 6:4
ECCLESIASTES 7:18

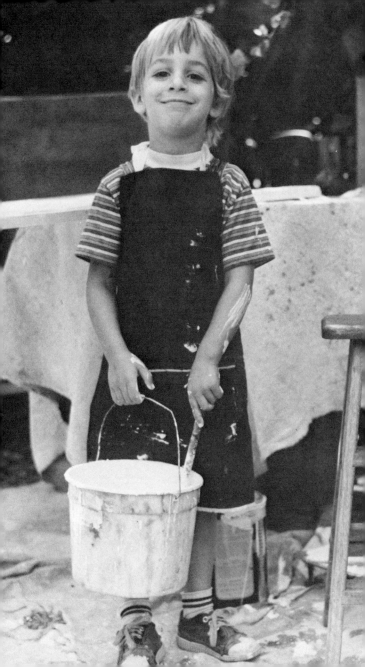

If you obey all of my commandments...

I will give you peace, and you will go to sleep without fear.

I will chase away the dangerous animals.

Kevin VanderKlay, age 7

I will look after you.

I will live among you.

For I am the Lord your God.

LEVITICUS 26:3, 6, 9, 11, 13

I lived before the earth began.

I lived before the oceans were created, before the springs bubbled forth their waters onto the earth, before the mountains and the hills were made.

I will be your God through all your lifetime, yes, even when your hair is white with age.

I made you and I will care for you.

PROVERBS 8:23, 24, 25   ISAIAH 46:4

MARCH
10

How dearly God loves us, and we feel this warm love everywhere within us.

God showed how much he loved us by sending his only Son into this wicked world to bring to us eternal life through his death.

Since God loved us as much as that, we surely ought to love each other.

ROMANS 5:5
1 JOHN 4:9, 11

Love comes from God.

Those who are loving and kind show that they are children of God, and that they are getting to know him better. But if a person isn't loving and kind, it shows that he doesn't know God—for God is love.

When we love each other, God lives in us and his love within us grows even stronger.

1 JOHN 4:7, 8, 12

When you do a kindness to someone, do it secretly.

And God, who knows all secrets, will reward you.

And if you give even a cup of cold water to a little child, you will surely be rewarded.

MATTHEW 6:3, 4   MATTHEW 10:42

Treat others as you want them to treat you.

Don't hold a grudge. But love your neighbor as yourself.

If you love your neighbor as much as you love yourself you will not want to harm or cheat him, or kill him, or steal from him.

Always be kind to everyone.

LUKE 6:31   LEVITICUS 19:18
ROMANS 13:9   GALATIANS 6:10

Love your enemies.

Pray for those who are mean to you. Don't say, "Now I can pay him back for all his meanness to me!"

If you love only those who love you, what good is that? If you are friendly only to your friends, how are you different from anyone else?

MATTHEW 5:44   PROVERBS 24:29
MATTHEW 5:46, 47

Follow God's example.

Be full of love for others, following
the example of Christ who loves
you.

Let us stop just *saying* we love
people. Let us *really* love them, and
show it by our actions. Then we
will know that we are on God's
side.

EPHESIANS 5:1, 2   1 JOHN 3:18, 19

What do you think about this?

A man with two sons told the older boy, "Son, go out and work on the farm today."

"I won't," he answered. But later he changed his mind and went.

Then the father told the youngest, "You go."

And he said, "Yes sir, I will." But he didn't.

Which of the two was obeying his father?

MATTHEW 21:28, 29, 30, 31

Christa Zapfe, age 8

Keep your lips from lying.

Stop lying to each other. Tell the truth. When we lie to each other we are hurting ourselves.

A good man is known by his truthfulness. God delights in those who keep their promises.

If you want a happy, good life, keep control of your tongue. Guard your lips from telling lies.

PSALM 34:13   EPHESIANS 4:25
PROVERBS 12:17, 22   1 PETER 3:10

The Lord hates the stubborn but delights in those who are good.

Don't be like a senseless horse or mule that has to have a bit in its mouth to keep it in line.

Anyone willing to be corrected is on the pathway to life.

If you search for good you will find God's favor.

PROVERBS 11:20   PSALM 32:9
PROVERBS 10:17   PROVERBS 11:27

I pray that you will live good lives.

For only good men enjoy life to the full.

Do you want more and more of God's kindness and peace? Then learn to know him better and better. He will give you everything you need for living a truly good life.

2 CORINTHIANS 13:7   PROVERBS 2:21
2 PETER 1:2, 3

Don't allow us to be tempted.

Temptation is the result of man's own evil thoughts and wishes.

Remember this: The wrong desires that come into your life aren't anything new and different. For we naturally love to do evil things.

Conquer evil by doing good.

LUKE 11:4   JAMES 1:14
1 CORINTHIANS 10:13
GALATIANS 5:17   ROMANS 12:21

Choose to love
the Lord your God.

We can choose the sounds we want
to listen to.

We can choose the taste we want
in food.

We should choose to follow what
is right.

Where is the man who honors
the Lord? God will teach him how
to choose the best. He shall live
within God's circle of blessing.

DEUTERONOMY 30:20   JOB 34:3, 4
PSALM 25:12, 13

Overlook my sins, O Lord!

Look at me through eyes of mercy and forgiveness, through eyes of everlasting love and kindness.

The Lord is good. He will teach the ways that are right and best to those who humbly turn to him.

PSALM 25:6, 7, 8, 9

The Lord loves those who try to be good.

Your attitude should be the kind that was shown us by Jesus Christ.

Don't be selfish. Don't live to make a good impression on others. Be humble, thinking of others as better than yourself.

Don't just think about your own business, but be interested in others, too, and in what they are doing.

PROVERBS 15:9   PHILIPPIANS 2:5, 3, 4

Be fair.

Be just and fair to all, the Lord God says. Do what's right and good. Treat others as you want them to treat you. Follow only what is good.

Remember that those who do what is right prove that they are God's children.

ZECHARIAH 8:16   ISAIAH 56:1   LUKE 6:31
3 JOHN 11

You will keep on guiding me all my life and afterwards receive me into the glories of heaven.

No one can hold back his spirit from departing. No one has the power to prevent his day of death.

When we die and leave these bodies we will have wonderful new bodies in heaven.

We will be at home with the Lord.

PSALM 73:24   ECCLESIASTES 8:8
2 CORINTHIANS 5:1, 8

I have created you and cared for you since you were born.

I will be your God through all your lifetime, yes, even when your hair is white with age. I made you and I will care for you. I will carry you along and be your Savior.

With what in all of heaven and earth do I compare? Whom can you find who equals me?

ISAIAH 46:3, 4, 5

MARCH 27

God has said, "I will never, *never* fail you nor leave you."

That is why we can say without any doubt or fear, "The Lord is my Helper and I am not afraid of anything that people can do to me." We need not fear even if the world blows up, and the mountains crumble into the sea.

HEBREWS 13:5, 6
PSALM 46:2

Ben Atkinson, age 9

God rules the world.

The soul of every living thing is in the hand of God. He alone rules over the earth.

God simply shatters the greatest of men, and puts others in their place.

PSALM 96:10   JOB 12:10   JOB 34:13, 24

Let everything God has made give praise to him.

For he spoke and they came into being.

Praise him, sun and moon, and all you twinkling stars. Praise him you creatures of the ocean depths.

Let fire and hail, snow, rain, wind and weather all obey.

PSALM 148:5, 3, 7, 8

Robin Brumley, age 8

We can see and understand only a little about God.

It is as if we were looking at his reflection in a poor mirror.

God's marvelous love is so great that you will never see the end of it or fully know or understand it. His greatness is beyond discovery.

1 CORINTHIANS 13:12   EPHESIANS 3:17, 19
PSALM 145:3

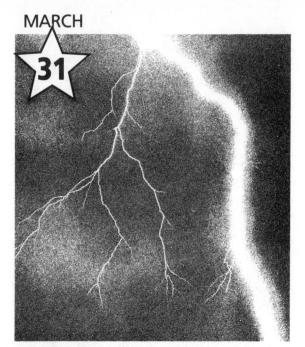

God is the Creator of all.

Our God formed the earth by his power and wisdom. By his intelligence he hung the stars in space and stretched out the heavens.

It is his voice that echoes in the thunder of the storm clouds. He causes mist to rise upon the earth. He sends the lightning and brings the rain.

JEREMIAH 10:16, 12, 13

Good News!

God makes us ready for heaven—
makes us right in God's sight—
when we put our faith and trust in
Christ to save us. And we all can be
saved in this same way no matter
who we are or what we have been
like. For God sent Christ Jesus to
take the punishment for our sins.

ROMANS 1:17   ROMANS 3:22, 25

If we say that we have no sin, we are only fooling ourselves.

When Adam sinned, sin entered the entire human race. As the Scriptures say, no one is good. All have sinned.

If we confess our sins to God, he can be depended on to forgive us and to cleanse us from every wrong.

1 JOHN 1:8   ROMANS 5:12   ROMANS 3:10, 23
1 JOHN 1:9

O Lord, I will praise you with all my heart.

I will tell everyone about the marvelous things you do. I will be glad, yes, filled with joy because of you. I will sing your praises, O Lord God.

You have taught the little children to praise you perfectly. May their example shame and silence your enemies.

PSALM 9:1, 2   PSALM 8:2

The Lord tells me what to do.

Samuel, though only a child, was the Lord's helper. He was helping the Lord by assisting Eli.

Make the most of every chance you have for doing good. Learn as you go along what pleases the Lord.

PSALM 16:7
1 SAMUEL 2:18
1 SAMUEL 3:1
EPHESIANS 5:15, 10

Hate evil and love the good.

Keep away from angry, short-tempered people, for fear that you will learn to be like them.

Live clean, innocent lives as children of God in a dark world full of people who are crooked and stubborn.

Don't let evil get the upper hand, but conquer evil by doing good.

AMOS 5:15   PROVERBS 22:24, 25
PHILIPPIANS 2:15   ROMANS 12:21

Work hard to be good.

But even that is not enough. You must learn to know God better and discover what he wants you to do.

Next, learn to put aside your own desires so that you will become patient and godly, gladly letting God have his way with you.

2 PETER 1:5, 6

Emily Showalter, age 9

Put on the armor of right living.

In a wealthy home there are dishes made of gold and silver as well as some made from wood and clay. The expensive dishes are used for guests, and the cheap ones are used in the kitchen or to put garbage in.

If you stay away from sin you will be like one of these dishes made of purest gold—the very best in the house.

ROMANS 13:12   2 TIMOTHY 2:20, 21

Be satisfied with what you have.

Then you won't need to look for honors and popularity, which lead to jealousy and hard feelings.

Let everyone be sure that he is doing his very best. For then he will have the personal satisfaction of work well done.

HEBREWS 13:5   GALATIANS 5:26
GALATIANS 6:4

Watch your tongue!

If you want a happy, good life, keep control of your tongue, and guard your lips from telling lies.

A good man hates lies. Wicked men lie constantly and come to shame.

PSALM 34:13   1 PETER 3:10   PROVERBS 13:5

APRIL
10

Don't try to act big.

When others are happy, be happy with them. If they are sad, share their sorrow. Work happily together.

Ask the Lord Jesus Christ to help you live as you should. For God is at work within you, helping you do what he wants.

ROMANS 12:16, 15, 16
ROMANS 13:14   PHILIPPIANS 2:13

APRIL

11

Use the skills God has given you.

Put these skills to work. Throw yourself into your tasks so that everyone may notice your improvement and progress.

To learn, you must want to be taught. Be lazy and never succeed.

1 TIMOTHY 4:14, 15   PROVERBS 12:1, 24

A lazy fellow has trouble all through life.

Lazy men are soon poor. Hard workers get rich.

A wise youth makes hay while the sun shines. But what a shame to see a lad who sleeps away his chance.

Work hard and become a leader. Be lazy and never succeed.

PROVERBS 15:19   PROVERBS 10:4, 5
PROVERBS 12:24

Lord, don't let me make a mess of things.

Keep me from getting into trouble.
How can I ever know what sins
are in my heart?
Cleanse me from these hidden

faults. And keep me
from wrongs that I do
on purpose. Help
me to stop doing
them.
PSALM 119:31
PSALM 32:7
PSALM 19:12, 13

Kristy Balke, age 8

Obey me and I will be your God.

Do as I say and all shall be well.

Happy are those who long to be just and good, for they shall be completely satisfied.

JEREMIAH 7:23   MATTHEW 5:6

The Lord delights in you.

The steps of good men are directed
by the Lord. He delights in each
step they take.

His joy is in those who reverence
him, those who expect him to be
loving and kind.

ISAIAH 62:4   PSALM 37:23   PSALM 147:11

APRIL

16

God is the supreme God of heaven.

I am God. There is no other.

You must not treat me as common and ordinary. For there is no other God but me—no, not one!

Let all the world look to me for salvation.

JOSHUA 2:11
ISAIAH 45:22
LEVITICUS 22:32
ISAIAH 45:21, 22

Kendra Perdue age 8

Salvation is within easy reach of us.

If you tell others with your own mouth that Jesus Christ is your Lord, and believe in your own heart that God has raised him from the dead, you will be saved.

DING DONG

Anyone who calls upon the name of the Lord will be saved.

ROMANS 10:8, 9, 13

Jeremy Botts, age 9

Diana Jeude, age 8

Now is the time to seek the Lord.

Come to the Lord and say, "O Lord, take away our sins. Be gracious to us and receive us."

And we all can be saved in this same way, by coming to Christ, no matter who we are or what we have been like.

HOSEA 10:12   ROMANS 3:22, 28

Tell God your needs.

Don't repeat the same prayer over and over. For God hears the cries of his needy ones, and does not look the other way. He will answer you.

Don't forget to thank him for his answers.

PHILIPPIANS 4:6   MATTHEW 6:7
PSALM 69:33   ISAIAH 30:19   PHILIPPIANS 4:6

APRIL

20

Your goodness and unfailing kindness shall be with me all of my life.

O Lord God, there is no one like you in heaven or earth. For you are loving and kind and you keep your promises to your people if they do their best to do your will.

O Lord, the earth is full of your love and kindness. You are good and do only good.

PSALM 23:6   1 KINGS 8:23   PSALM 119:64

Let everything he has made give praise to God.

For he spoke and they came into being.

Let the sea in all its vastness roar with praise. Let the waves clap their hands in glee, and the hills sing out their songs of joy before the Lord.

PSALM 148:5, 3   PSALM 98:7, 8, 9

How God loves his people.

O Lord, you are so good and kind,
so ready to forgive, so full of mercy
for all who ask your help.

You love me so much. You are
constantly so kind. You are
merciful and gentle, full of
constant love and kindness and
truth.

DEUTERONOMY 33:3   PSALM 86:5, 13, 15

God himself is teaching you to love one another.

Love is very patient and kind, never jealous or bossy, never boastful or proud, never stuck-up or selfish or rude.

Love does not demand its own way. It is not quarrelsome or touchy. It does not hold grudges.

1 THESSALONIANS 4:9   1 CORINTHIANS 13:4, 5

Loribeth VanDerMolen, age 6

Don't think only of yourself.

You must love and help your
neighbors.

Try to think of the other person,
and what is best for him.

Don't pay back evil for evil. Don't
snap back at those who say unkind
things about you. Instead, pray for
God's help for them. For we are to
be kind to others.

1 CORINTHIANS 10:24   JAMES 2:8
1 CORINTHIANS 10:24   1 PETER 3:9

Say only what is good and helpful to those you are talking to.

Don't use bad language.

The tongue is a small thing, but what great damage it can do! As surely as a wind from the north brings cold, just as surely talking back causes anger.

Watch your tongue!

EPHESIANS 4:29   JAMES 3:5
PROVERBS 25:23   PSALM 34:13

Others will treat you as you treat them.

Stop being mean, bad-tempered, and angry. Quarreling, unkind words, and dislike of others should have no place in your lives. Instead be kind to each other. Be like one big happy family.

MATTHEW 7:2   EPHESIANS 4:31, 32   1 PETER 3:8

Students are wise who master what their teachers tell them.

Work hard so God can say to you, "Well done."

Throw yourself into your tasks so that everyone may notice your improvement and progress.

Don't let anyone think little of you because you are young.

ECCLESIASTES 12:11
1 TIMOTHY 4:15, 12
2 TIMOTHY 2:15

A wicked man is always in trouble.

You can be very sure that the evil man will not go unpunished.

The wicked shall lose everything. His fears will all come true.

The good man can look forward to happiness.

JOB 15:20   PROVERBS 11:21   PROVERBS 10:30, 24
PROVERBS 11:23

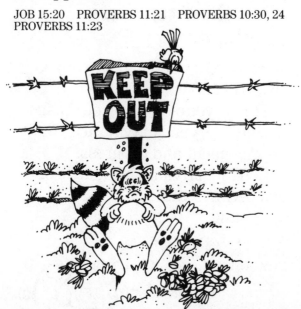

Katie Gieser, age 7

Happy are those who long to be just and good.

Only good people enjoy life to the full. Evil people lose the good things they might have had and they themselves shall be destroyed.

The person who tries to be good, loving, and kind finds life, righteousness, and honor.

MATTHEW 5:6   PROVERBS 2:21, 22
PROVERBS 21:21

The godly person's life is exciting.

Fix your thoughts on what is true and good and right. Think about things that are pure and lovely. Dwell on the fine, good things in others. Think about all you can praise God for and be glad about.

For only good people enjoy life to the full.

PROVERBS 14:14   PHILIPPIANS 4:8
PROVERBS 2:21

What a wonderful God!

O Lord my God, many and many a time you have done great miracles for us. We are ever in your thoughts. Who else can do such marvelous things? No one else can be compared with you!

How wonderful it is, Lord, to realize that you are thinking about me constantly! I can't even count how many times a day your thoughts turn toward me.

ROMANS 11:33   PSALM 40:5   PSALM 139:17, 18

Because the Lord is my Shepherd, I have everything I need!

He lets me rest in the grass and leads me beside the quiet streams. He restores my failing health. He helps me do what honors him the most.

Even when walking through the dark valley of death I will not be afraid, for you are close beside me, guarding, guiding all the way.

PSALM 23:1, 2, 3, 4

Let not your heart be troubled.

I will not leave you alone in storm. I will come to you.

I am with you always, even to the end of the world. I will never, *never* fail you nor leave you.

That is why you can say without any doubt or fear, "The Lord is my Helper."

Debby Dvorak, age 8

JOHN 14:1, 18
MATTHEW 28:20
HEBREWS 13:5, 6

MAY

4

The Lord is my Helper.

He helps me do what honors him
the most.

He is for me. The Lord is on my
side. He will help me. He even
keeps me from getting into trouble.

HEBREWS 13:6   PSALM 23:3   PSALM 118:6, 7
PSALM 32:7

Listen carefully now to all these laws God has given you.

Learn them and be sure to obey them.

It always goes well with us when we obey all the laws of the Lord our God. So keep these commandments carefully in mind.

DEUTERONOMY 5:1   DEUTERONOMY 6:25
DEUTERONOMY 11:18

MAY

6

God's law is "Honor your father and mother."

You children must always obey your fathers and mothers, for that pleases the Lord.

Tie their instructions around your finger so you won't forget. Take to heart all of their advice. Every day and all night long their direction will lead you and save you from harm.

MATTHEW 15:4
COLOSSIANS 3:20
PROVERBS 6:21, 22

May God help you to live in complete harmony with each other.

No one will recognize the tune the flute is playing unless each note is sounded clearly.

Stop arguing among yourselves. Let there be real harmony. You should be like one big happy family.

ROMANS 15:5   1 CORINTHIANS 14:7
1 CORINTHIANS 1:10   1 PETER 3:8

Don't eavesdrop!

Don't let me hear of your making trouble or being a busybody and snooping into other people's business.

Live in peace with each other.

How wonderful it is, how pleasant, when brothers live in harmony!

ECCLESIASTES 7:21
1 PETER 4:15
MARK 9:50
PSALM 133:1

9

Love does no wrong to anyone.

If you love people, you will be obeying all of God's laws. You won't do anything the Ten Command-ments say is wrong.

That's why love fully satisfies all of God's demands. It is the only law you need.

ROMANS 13:10, 8, 9, 10

WOW! THE TEACHER LEFT OUT THE ANSWERS TO TOMORROW'S TEST

I have chosen to do right.

Lord, don't let me make a mess of things. Just tell me what to do and I will do it. As long as I live I'll obey.

Turn me away from wanting any other plan than yours.

PSALM 119:29, 31, 33, 34, 37

God will give you all your heart's desires.

Commit everything you do to the Lord. Trust him to help you do it and he will.

Let him have all your worries and cares. For he is always thinking about you and watching everything that concerns you.

PSALM 37:4, 5   1 PETER 5:7

**O Lord God!
Nothing is
too hard for you!**

You have made the heavens and earth by your great power.

You have all wisdom and do great and mighty miracles. Your eyes are open to all the ways of men. You reward everyone according to his life and deeds.

You have made your name very great.

JEREMIAH 32:17, 19, 20

13 God is in supreme charge of all the earth.

He waters the earth to make it green. Showers soften the earth causing seeds to grow across the land. Then he crowns it all with green, lush pastures.

The pastures are filled with flocks of sheep, and the valleys are carpeted with grain.

All the world shouts with joy and sings!

PSALM 65:9, 10, 11, 13

MAY

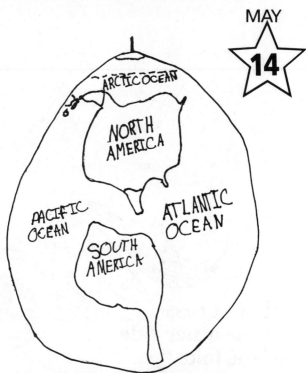

Jason Willcutt, age 8

These are some of the minor things God does:

God stretches out heaven over empty space, and hangs the earth upon nothing.

God wraps the rain in his thick clouds, and the clouds are not split by the weight.

God sets a limit for the ocean. By his power the sea grows calm.

JOB 26:14, 7, 8, 10, 12

"Let's cross to the other side of the lake."

A terrible storm arose. High waves began to break into the boat until it was nearly full of water and about to sink.

He spoke to the wind and said to the sea, "Quiet down!" And the wind fell and there was a great calm.

And they said, "Who is this man, that even the winds and seas obey him?"

MARK 4:35, 37, 39, 41

The sailors sailing the seven seas observe the power of God in action.

He calls to the storm winds. The waves rise high. The sailors shake in terror.

Then they cry to the Lord in their trouble, and he saves them. He calms the storm and stills the waves. He brings them safely into harbor.

PSALM 107:23, 24, 25, 26, 28, 29, 30

The earth breaks out in praise to God!

Sing your praise accompanied by music from the harp. Let the cornets and trumpets shout!

Let the sea in all its vastness roar with praise! Let the earth and all those living on it shout, "Glory to the Lord."

Let the waves clap their hands in glee, and the hills sing out their songs of joy!

PSALM 98:4, 5, 6, 7, 8, 9

I will not leave you or fail to help you.

The Lord your God is with you wherever you go. Nothing will ever be able to separate you from the love of God.

The Lord will guide you continually, and satisfy you with all good things, and keep you healthy too.

Leslie Horton, age 6

JOSHUA 1:5, 9   ROMANS 8:39   ISAIAH 58:11

Don't worry.

Look at the birds. They don't worry about what to eat. Your heavenly Father feeds them. And you are far more valuable to him than they are.

So don't be fearful about tomorrow.

MATTHEW 6:25, 26, 34

I will keep on expecting God to help me.

O God, you have helped me from my earliest childhood. You have been with me from birth and have helped me constantly. When I am afraid I will put my hope in you. Yes, I will trust the promises of God.

This one thing I know: God is for me!

PSALM 71:14, 17, 6   PSALM 56:3, 4, 9

Doran Stambaugh, age 9

I want you always to see clearly the difference between right and wrong.

The Lord shows us the difference between right and wrong.

- A good man hates lies. Wicked men lie constantly.
- A man's goodness helps him all through life. Evil men are being destroyed by their wickedness.

PHILIPPIANS 1:10   PROVERBS 2:9
PROVERBS 13:5, 6

What hope has the godless?

Will God listen to his cry when trouble comes upon him?

God is a judge who is perfectly fair. And he is angry with the wicked every day.

Though the godless person be proud as the heavens, and walk with his nose in the air, yet he shall die forever.

Never be jealous of the wicked.

JOB 27:8, 9   PSALM 7:11   JOB 20:6, 7   PSALM 37:1

Mitchell Freeman, age 8

The godly learn by watching ruin destroy the wicked.

Sin is deep in the hearts of the wicked, forever wanting them to do evil deeds. They have no fear of God. They think they can hide their evil deeds and not get caught.

Never be jealous of the wicked. For the wicked shall be destroyed. But those who trust the Lord shall be given every blessing.

PROVERBS 21:12   PSALM 36:1, 2, 3   PSALM 37:1, 9

God will protect his godly ones.

He grants good sense to the godly—his saints. He is their shield, protecting them and guarding their pathway.

He shows how to tell the difference between right and wrong, how to find the right decision every time.

Only good men enjoy life to the full. Evil men lose the good things they might have had.

1 SAMUEL 2:9   PROVERBS 2:7, 8, 21, 22

Keep me far from every wrong.

Help me to obey your laws. For I have chosen to do right.

I cling to your commands and follow them as closely as I can.

Lord, don't let me make a mess of things. If you will only help me to want your will, then I will follow your laws even more closely.

PSALM 119:29, 30, 31, 32

The character of even a child can be known by the way he acts— whether what he does is pure and right.

If you must choose, take a good name rather than great riches. To be loved is better than silver and gold.

Practice loving each other. For love comes from God. Those who are loving and kind show that they are the children of God and that they are getting to know him better.'

PROVERBS 20:11   ECCLESIASTES 7:1   1 JOHN 4:7

Love each other with brotherly love.

The Lord asked Cain, "Where is your brother? Where is Abel?"

"How should I know?" Cain replied. "Am I supposed to keep track of him wherever he goes?"

You should be like one big happy family, full of sympathy toward each other, loving one another with tender hearts and humble minds.

ROMANS 12:10   GENESIS 4:9   1 PETER 3:8

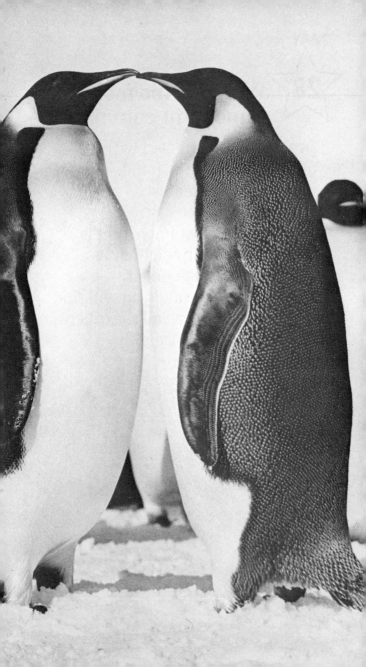

Which is the most important command?

Love the Lord your God with all your heart, soul, and mind. This is the first and greatest commandment.

The second most important is similar: Love your neighbor as much as you love yourself.

Keep only these and you will find that you are obeying all the others.

MATTHEW 22:36, 37, 38, 39, 40

The little boy greatly loved God.

Jesus said, "Let the little children come to me. For of such is the Kingdom of Heaven."

I love all who love me. Those who search for me shall surely find me.

Listen to me, for how happy are all who follow my instructions.

LUKE 1:80   MATTHEW 19:14
PROVERBS 8:17   PROVERBS 8:32

The Lord delights in honesty.

Daniel was faithful and honest. So Daniel prospered.

You know what God wants. You know right from wrong. Do things in such a way that everyone can see you are honest clear through.

PROVERBS 11:1   DANIEL 6:3, 4, 28
ROMANS 2:18   ROMANS 12:17

Keep your promise.

It is far better not to say you'll do something than to say you will and then not do it.

So when you talk to God and say that you will do something, don't delay in doing it.

The Lord delights in those who keep their promises.

ECCLESIASTES 5:4, 5, 4   PROVERBS 12:22

JUNE 1

God will reward everyone according to his deeds.

The righteous person will be rewarded for his own goodness and the wicked person for his wickedness.

But if a wicked person turns away from all his sins and begins to obey God's laws and do what is just and right, all his past sins will be forgotten. He shall live because of his goodness.

PROVERBS 24:12
EZEKIEL 18:20, 21, 22

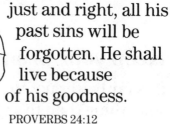

Jeremy Botts, age 9

ALL HAVE GONE WRONG

There is not a single person in all the earth who is always good and never sins.

As the Scriptures say, "No one is good. No one in all the world is innocent." But if we confess our sins to God, he can be depended on to forgive us.

ROMANS 3:12 ECCLESIASTES 7:20
ROMANS 3:10 1 JOHN 1:9

God will give eternal life.

The free gift of God is eternal life through Jesus Christ our Lord.

Anyone who believes in God, even though he dies like anyone else, shall live again.

He is given eternal life.

ROMANS 2:7   ROMANS 6:23   JOHN 11:25, 26

It is good to say, "Thank you" to the Lord.

Every morning tell him, "Thank you for your kindness." Every evening rejoice in all his faithfulness.

Thank God for his Son—his Gift too wonderful for words.

Say "Thank you" to the Lord for being so good, for always being so loving and kind. Thank the Lord for all the wonderful things he does.

PSALM 92:1, 2   2 CORINTHIANS 9:15
PSALM 107:1   PSALM 105:1

Everything comes from God alone.

God has given you the seed-bearing plants all over the earth, and all the fruit trees for your food. And God has given all the grass and plants to the animals and birds for their food. All wild animals and birds and fish are yours to use for food, in addition to grain and vegetables.

He gives food to those who trust him. He never forgets his promises.

ROMANS 11:36   GENESIS 1:29
GENESIS 9:2   PSALM 111:5

Katie Gieser, age 7

God placed springs in the valleys, and streams that gush from the mountains.

They give water for all the animals to drink. There the wild donkeys satisfy their thirst. The birds nest beside the streams and sing among the branches of the trees.

They all depend on you to give them daily food. You supply it. They are satisfied.

PSALM 104:10, 11, 12, 27, 28

JUNE

7

God is concerned for men and animals alike.

Who makes the wild donkeys wild? God has placed them in the wilderness. For they hate the noise of the city.

Who provides for the ravens when their young cry out to God and they try to struggle up from their nest in hunger?

Look at the birds. Your heavenly Father feeds them. And you are far more valuable to him than they are.

PSALM 36:6   JOB 39:5, 6, 7
JOB 38:41   MATTHEW 6:26

Because the Lord is my Shepherd, I have everything I need!

You provide delicious food for me in the presence of my enemies. You have welcomed me as your guest. Blessings overflow!

Your goodness and unfailing kindness shall be with me all of my life, and afterwards I will live with you forever in your home.

PSALM 23:1, 5, 6

9

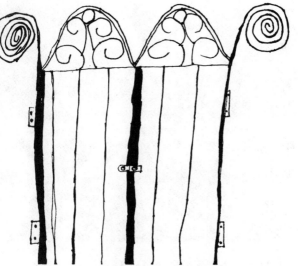

Dirk Bosgraf, age 9

God will open wide the gate of heaven.

There are many homes up there where my Father lives. I, Christ, am going to prepare them for your coming.

God has reserved for his children the priceless gift of eternal life. It is kept in heaven for you.

For this world is not our home.

2 PETER 1:11   JOHN 14:2
1 PETER 1:4   HEBREWS 13:14

There is a time for everything.

No one can hold back his spirit from departing. No one has the power to prevent his day of death.

We are not afraid to die for then we will be at home with the Lord. God will give us new bodies— bodies that will never be sick again and will never die.

All that happens to us is working for our good.

ECCLESIASTES 8:6, 8
2 CORINTHIANS 5:8   ROMANS 8:23, 28

Todd Hoskins, age 9

Never forget the things I've taught you.

If you want a long and satisfying life, closely follow my instructions. Never forget to be truthful and kind.

If you want favor with both God and man, trust the Lord completely.

In everything you do, put God first, and he will direct you and crown your efforts with success.

PROVERBS 3:1, 2, 3, 4, 5, 6

Don't be quick-tempered. That is being a fool.

Stop being mean, bad-tempered, and angry. Quarreling, unkind words, and dislike of others should have no place in your life.

Ask the Lord Jesus to help you live as you should.

ECCLESIASTES 7:9   EPHESIANS 4:31
ROMANS 13:14

The policeman is sent by God to help you.

The policeman does not frighten people who are doing right. But those doing evil will always fear him.

So if you don't want to be afraid, keep the laws and you will get along well. But if you are doing something wrong, of course you should be afraid, for the policeman will have you punished. He is sent by God for that very purpose.

ROMANS 13:4, 3, 4

JUNE

14

Happy is the man who doesn't give in and do wrong.

Temptation is the result of man's own evil thoughts and wishes. For we naturally love to do evil things. Temptation to do wrong will come.

The Lord can rescue you and me from the temptations that surround us.

Conquer evil by doing good.

JAMES 1:12, 14   GALATIANS 5:17
2 PETER 2:9   ROMANS 12:21

**Don't be fooled
by those who try
to excuse these sins:**

- *QUARRELING*
- Being *JEALOUS* of each other
- Being *ANGRY* with each other
- Acting *BIG*
- Saying *WICKED* things
about each other
- *WHISPERING*
behind each other's backs

That isn't the way Christ taught you. Your attitudes and thoughts must all be constantly changing for the better.

EPHESIANS 5:6 2 CORINTHIANS 12:20
EPHESIANS 4:20, 23

JUNE

16

**Quietly
trust
in the
Lord—
now,
and
always.**

Trusting means looking forward to
getting something we don't yet
have. It teaches us to wait patiently.

Just as you trusted Christ to save
you, trust him, too, for each day's
problems.

PSALM 131:3   ROMANS 8:24, 25   COLOSSIANS 2:6

Andy Oury, age 7

Listen to your father and mother.

Take to heart all of their advice. Every day and all night long their direction will lead you and save you from harm.

When you wake up in the morning, let their instructions guide you into the new day.

PROVERBS 1:8   PROVERBS 6:21, 22

Happy are all who perfectly follow the laws of God.

God's laws are perfect. They protect us, make us wise, and give us joy and light.

God's laws are more desirable than gold. For they warn us away from harm and give success to those who obey them.

Happy are all who hear the Word of God and put it into practice.

PSALM 119:1   PSALM 19:7, 8, 9, 10, 11   LUKE 11:28

The Lord will give you lots of good things.

Your heavenly Father will give them to you if you give him first place in your life and live as he wants you to.

No man has ever seen, heard, or even imagined what wonderful things God has ready for those who love the Lord.

DEUTERONOMY 28:11   MATTHEW 6:33
1 CORINTHIANS 2:9

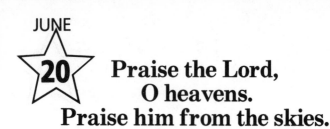

JUNE

20

Praise the Lord, O heavens. Praise him from the skies.

Praise him down here on earth, you creatures of the ocean depths. Let fire and hail, snow, rain, wind and weather, all obey. Let the mountains and hills, the fruit trees and cedars, the wild animals and cattle, the snakes and birds, the kings and all the people, with their rulers and judges, young men and women, old men and children —all praise the Lord together.

PSALM 148:7, 8, 9, 10, 11, 12

Heather Oleari, age 7

By my great power I have made the earth and all mankind and every animal.

Who makes the wild donkeys wild?

Do you know how a hawk soars and spreads her wings to the south?

Who provides for the ravens when their young cry out to God?

O Lord, what a variety you have made!

JEREMIAH 27:5   JOB 39:5, 26   JOB 38:41
PSALM 104:24

God made all sorts of wild animals.

Can you catch leviathan with a hook and line? Can you make a pet of him like a bird? His teeth are terrible. Iron is nothing but straw to him.

If you lay your hands upon him, you will long remember the battle that takes place. You will never try it again!

There is nothing else so fearless anywhere on earth.

GENESIS 1:25   JOB 41:1, 5, 14, 27, 8, 33

The Lord gives the farmer wisdom.

Is the farmer forever plowing the soil and never planting it?

Does he not finally plant his many kinds of grain, each in its own section of his land?

He knows just what to do, for God has made him see and understand.

ISAIAH 28:29, 24, 25, 26

"Lord, teach us a prayer to recite."

This is the prayer:

"Father, may your name be honored for its holiness.

Send your Kingdom soon.

Give us our food day by day.

And forgive us our sins. For we have forgiven those who sinned against us.

And don't allow us to be tempted."

LUKE 11:1, 2, 3, 4

The rain came down. The water covered the earth for 150 days.

God didn't forget about Noah and all the animals in the boat. He sent a wind to blow across the waters, and the floods began to disappear.

God told Noah, "I will never again send another flood to destroy the earth. I have placed my rainbow in the clouds as a sign of my promise."

GENESIS 9:8, 11, 13

Obey your parents.

This is the right thing to do because God has placed them in authority over you.

Take to heart all of their advice. Every day and all night long their direction will lead you and save you from harm.

Give your parents joy.

EPHESIANS 6:1   PROVERBS 6:21, 22
PROVERBS 23:25

The Lord loved the baby.

Children are a gift from God. They are his reward.

Jesus took the children into his arms and placed his hands on their heads and he blessed them.

Don't look down upon a single one of these little children. In heaven their angels are right there with God.

2 SAMUEL 10:24   PSALM 127:3
MARK 10:16   MATTHEW 18:10

God wants his loved ones to get their proper rest.

You need not be afraid of disaster. For the Lord is with you. He protects you.

Don't worry about anything. Instead, pray about everything. Tell God your needs. And don't forget to thank him for his answers.

I will lie down in peace and sleep. For though I am alone, O Lord, you will keep me safe.

PSALM 127:2   PROVERBS 3:24, 25, 26
PHILIPPIANS 4:6   PSALM 4:8

All who listen to God shall live in peace and safety, unafraid.

We need not fear even if the world blows up, and the mountains crumble into the sea.

We live within the shadow of the Almighty, sheltered by the God who is above all gods.

You need not be afraid of disaster. The Lord is with you. He protects you.

PROVERBS 1:33   PSALM 46:2
PSALM 91:1   PROVERBS 3:25, 26

Joel Kubin, age 9

God is a judge who is perfectly fair.

The Lord rules from heaven. He closely watches everything that happens here on earth.

You can be very sure that the evil man will not go unpunished. And you can also be sure that God will rescue the children of the godly. The good man can look forward to happiness, while the wicked can expect only anger.

PSALM 7:11   PSALM 11:4   PROVERBS 11:21, 23

There are six things the Lord hates— no seven.

1. Pride
2. Lying
3. Murdering
4. Plotting evil
5. Eagerness to do wrong
6. A false witness
7. Quarreling among brothers.

For God is good. He loves whatever is just and good.

PROVERBS 6:16, 17, 18, 19   PSALM 11:7
PSALM 33:5

God is always watching, never sleeping.

Jehovah himself
is caring for you.
He is your defender.
He protects you
day and night.
He keeps you.
from all evil.
He keeps his eye
upon you as
you come and go,
and always guards you.

PSALM 121:4, 5, 6, 7, 8

JULY
3

God is not one who likes things to be out of order and upset.

Work happily together. Be at peace with one another.

Whatever you do, do well. Never be lazy.

This should be your desire: to live a quiet life, minding your own business.

1 CORINTHIANS 14:33   ROMANS 12:16
EPHESIANS 4:3   ECCLESIASTES 9:10
ROMANS 12:11   1 THESSALONIANS 4:11

Practice loving each other.

Don't just pretend that you love others, *really* love them. Hate what is wrong. Stand on the side of the good. Love each other.

Love does not demand its own way. It is not quarrelsome or touchy. It does not hold grudges.

1 JOHN 4:7   ROMANS 12:9, 10
1 CORINTHIANS 13:4, 5

Don't let evil get the upper hand, but conquer evil by doing good.

Don't repay evil for evil. Don't snap back at those who say unkind things about you. Instead, pray for God's help for them. For we are to be kind to others. God will bless us for it.

ROMANS 12:21   1 PETER 3:9

Tackle every task that comes along.

Never be lazy in your work.

In a race, everyone runs but only one person gets first prize. So run your race to win.

Whatever you do, do well.

ECCLESIASTES 7:18   ROMANS 12:11
PHILIPPIANS 3:14   ECCLESIASTES 9:10

Take a lesson from the ants.

They aren't strong but they store
up food for the winter. They have
no king to make them work, yet
they work hard all summer,
gathering food for the winter.

Throw yourself into your tasks.
Be sure everything is done properly
in a good and orderly way.

PROVERBS 6:6   PROVERBS 30:25
PROVERBS 6:7   1 TIMOTHY 4:15
1 CORINTHIANS 14:40

God is my helper.

He is a friend of mine. He is for me. How can I be afraid? What can people do to me?

The Lord is on my side. He will help me.

My health fails. Yet God remains. He is the strength of my heart.

PSALM 54:4   PSALM 118:6, 7   PSALM 73:26

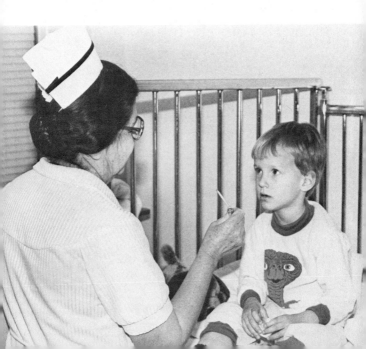

God is good.

Whatever is good and perfect
comes to us from God. He is good to
everyone. When trouble comes, he
is the place to go. And he knows
everyone who trusts in him. For
God is love.

PSALM 11:7   JAMES 1:17   PSALM 145:9
NAHUM 1:7   1 JOHN 4:8

All that happens to us is working for our good if we love God.

Let him have all your worries and cares, for he is always thinking about you and watching everything that concerns you.

If God is on our side, who can ever be against us? Nothing can ever separate us from his love.

ROMANS 8:28
1 PETER 5:7
ROMANS 8:31, 38

Heaven and earth shall disappear,
but God's words stand sure forever.
For every promise from God shall
surely come true.

Oh, the joys of those who delight
in doing everything God wants
them to, and day and night are
always thinking about ways to
follow him more closely.

ISAIAH 40:8   MATTHEW 13:31   LUKE 1:37   PSALM 1:1, 2

The Word of our God shall stand forever.

God heard my prayer! He paid attention to it!

Oh, thank the Lord, for he's so good!

The Lord is always good. He is always loving and kind. His faithfulness goes on and on.

Let everyone bless God and sing his praises, for he holds our lives in his hands.

PSALM 66:19   PSALM 118:1
PSALM 100:5   PSALM 66:8, 9

JULY 13

You are the God in charge of all the earth.

Everything in the heavens and earth is yours, O Lord, and this is your kingdom. We adore you as being in control of everything.

Riches and honor come from you alone. You are the Ruler of all mankind. Your hand controls power and might. At your word men are made great and given strength.   PSALM 83:18   1 CHRONICLES 29:11, 12

Day and night belong to you.

You made the starlight and the sun. All nature is within your hands.

As a shepherd leads his sheep, calling each by its pet name, and counts them to see that none are lost or strayed, so God does with stars and planets.

Can you say that the Lord doesn't see your troubles and isn't being fair?

PSALM 74:16, 17   ISAIAH 40:26, 27

This great God will be our guide until we die.

He will feed his flock like a shepherd. He will carry the lambs in his arms and gently lead the ewes with young.

He calls his own sheep by name and leads them out. He walks ahead of them. They follow him, for they recognize his voice.

We are God's sheep. He is our Shepherd.

PSALM 48:14   ISAIAH 40:11   JOHN 10:3, 4
PSALM 95:7

God will not fail to help you.

God doesn't change his mind like humans do. He never forgets his promises.

He is a mighty Savior. He will love you.

NUMBERS 23:19   PSALM 111:5
ZEPHANIAH 3:17, 18

Colleen Rehr, age 6

The Father himself loves us dearly.

We know how dearly God loves us, and we feel this warm love everywhere within us because God has given us the Holy Spirit to fill our hearts with his love.

Nothing will ever be able to separate us from the love of God.

JOHN 16:27   ROMANS 5:5   ROMANS 8:39

Love one another.

If we love God, we will do whatever he tells us to. And he has told us from the very first to love each other.

Love is never jealous or bossy, never boastful or proud, never stuck-up or selfish or rude. Love does not demand its own way.

2 JOHN 5, 6   1 CORINTHIANS 13:4, 5

You can have real love for everyone.

Obey our Lord's command. Love each other with brotherly love.

Love and help your neighbors just as much as you love and take care of yourself.

Whenever we can we should always be kind to everyone.

1 PETER 1:22   JAMES 2:8   ROMANS 12:10
JAMES 2:8   GALATIANS 6:10

Happy are the kind and merciful.

The man who tries to be good, loving, and kind finds life, righteousness, and honor.

God has told you what he wants, and this is all it is: to be fair and just and merciful, and to walk humbly with your God.

MATTHEW 5:7   PROVERBS 21:21   MICAH 6:8

Let everyone be sure that he is doing his very best.

It's wonderful to be young! Enjoy every minute of it! Do all you want to. Take in everything. But realize that you are responsible to God for everything you do.

Whatever you do, do well. Never be lazy in your work.

GALATIANS 6:4   ECCLESIASTES 11:9
ECCLESIASTES 9:10   ROMANS 12:11

Learn to be wise.

All who listen to Jesus' instructions and follow them are wise, like a man who builds his house on solid rock.

The rain comes down. The floods rise. The storm winds beat against his house. But it won't fall, for it is built on rock.

A wise man is careful and avoids danger.

PROVERBS 4:5
MATTHEW 7:24, 25
PROVERBS 14:16

The fool tries to fool himself and won't face facts.

Those who hear Jesus' instructions and ignore them are foolish, like a man who builds his house on sand.

For when the rains and floods come and storm winds beat against his house, it will fall with a mighty crash.

A fool goes ahead with great confidence. A wise man is careful and avoids danger.

MATTHEW 7:26, 27
PROVERBS 14:8
PROVERBS 14:16

JULY

24

The wise man learns by listening.

The Lord came and called, "Samuel! Samuel!" And Samuel replied, "Yes, I'm listening."

Sons and daughters, come and listen and let me teach you the importance of trusting and fearing the Lord.

Listen to your father's advice.

PROVERBS 21:11   1 SAMUEL 3:10
PSALM 34:11   PROVERBS 23:22

Ignore God's Word and find yourself in trouble.
Obey it and succeed.

Listen to God's instructions. For all God's words are right.

- They protect us.
- They make us wise.
- They keep us from harm.
- They give success to those who obey them.

PROVERBS 13:13   JOB 22:22
PSALM 33:4   PSALM 19:8, 11

We were born but yesterday and know so little.

But the wisdom of the past will teach you.

The experience of others will speak to you, reminding you that those who forget God have no hope. They are like grass without water to keep it alive.

JOB 8:9, 10, 11, 12, 13

Get all the help you can.

Remember your leaders who have taught you the Word of God. Think of all the good that has come from their lives. Try to trust the Lord as they do. Be willing to do what they say.

For all God's words are right.

HEBREWS 13:7, 17   PROVERBS 23:12   PSALM 33:4

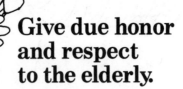

Give due honor and respect to the elderly.

Never speak sharply to an older man. Treat the older women as mothers.

Let us not get tired of doing what is right. Whenever we can, we should always be kind to everyone.

LEVITICUS 19:32   1 TIMOTHY 5:1, 2
GALATIANS 6:9, 10

We are all created equal by the same God.

One's nationality or race or education or social position is not important. The rich and poor are alike before the Lord, who made them all.

He doesn't care how great a man may be and he doesn't pay more attention to the rich than to the poor.

MALACHI 2:10   COLOSSIANS 3:11
PROVERBS 22:2   JOB 34:19

You made my body, Lord.

You made all the delicate, inner parts of my body.

Thank you for making me so wonderfully complex. It is amazing to think about! Your workmanship is marvelous.

You saw me before I was born and planned every day of my life before I began to breathe.

PSALM 119:73   PSALM 139:13, 14, 16

Kristy Kunard, age 6

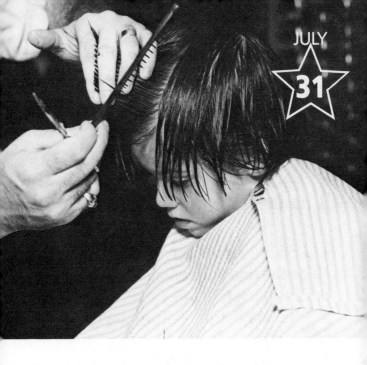

God knows the secrets of every heart.

The very hairs of your head are all numbered. He knows about everyone, everywhere. Everything about us is bare and wide open to the all-seeing eyes of our living God.

Day by day the Lord sees the good deeds done by godly men and gives them eternal rewards.

PSALM 44:21   MATTHEW 10:30
HEBREWS 4:13   PSALM 37:18

The earth belongs to God.

Everything in all the world is his. He is the one who pushed the oceans back to let dry land appear.

Who may stand before the Lord? Only those with pure hands and hearts, who do not practice dishonesty and lying.

These are the ones who are allowed to stand before the Lord and worship the God of Jacob.

PSALM 24:1, 2, 3, 4, 6

How can a man be truly good in the eyes of God?

God makes us right in his sight when we put our faith and trust in Christ to save us.

As the Scripture says it, "The man who finds life will find it through trusting God."

JOB 9:2   ROMANS 1:17

This Good News was promised long ago.

It is the Good News about Jesus Christ our Lord, who came as a human baby. By being raised from the dead he was proved to be the mighty Son of God.

This Good News tells us that God makes us ready for heaven—makes us right in God's sight—when we put our faith and trust in Christ to save us.

ROMANS 1:2, 3, 4, 17

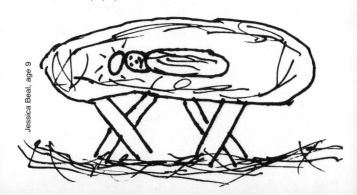

Jessica Beal, age 9

AUGUST
4

Cassandra VanDerMolen, age 7

God chose me to be his very own.

Even before I was born God had chosen me to be his.

His unchanging plan has always been to adopt me into his family by sending Jesus Christ to die for me. And he did this because he wanted to!

EPHESIANS 1:4   GALATIANS 1:15
EPHESIANS 1:5

I will not forget the wonderful things God does for me.

He forgives all my sins.
He surrounds me with love.
He fills my life with good things.
He is my God.
He is my Shepherd.
The Lord is a great God.

PSALM 103:2, 3, 4, 5   PSALM 95:7, 3

All the earth shall worship you and sing of your glories.

The earth breaks out in praise to God and sings for joy.

The earth and all those living on it shout, "Glory to the Lord."

The waves clap their hands in glee. The hills sing out their songs of joy. The trees in the woods sing for joy before the Lord.

PSALM 66:4   PSALM 98:4, 7, 8
1 CHRONICLES 16:33

God is a friend of mine.

Friendship with God is saved for those who reverence him.

His mercy toward those who fear and honor him is as great as the height of the heavens above the earth.

He is like a father to us, tender and understanding to those who reverence him. His joy is in those who expect him to be loving and kind.

PSALM 54:4   PSALM 25:14   PSALM 103:11, 13
PSALM 147:11

AUGUST

8 Don't worry about anything.

If my mother and father should leave me, you would welcome and comfort me.

You love me. You are holding my right hand. You will keep on guiding me all my life with your wisdom and direction. And afterwards you will receive me into the glories of heaven.

PSALM 48:14   PSALM 27:10   PSALM 73:23, 24

This great God is our God forever and ever.

God is always thinking about you and watching everything that concerns you.

He is always watching, never sleeping.

He has created you and cared for you since you were born. He will be your God through all your lifetime.

PHILIPPIANS 4:6   1 PETER 5:7
PSALM 121:4   ISAIAH 46:3

I am trusting him.

I will lie down in peace and sleep. For though I am alone, O Lord, you will keep me safe.

O God, listen to me. Hear my prayer. For you are a high tower where my enemies can never reach me. Oh, to be safe beneath the shelter of your wings.

Then I lay down and slept in peace and woke up safely, for the Lord was watching over me.

PSALM 91:2   PSALM 4:8   PSALM 61:1, 3, 4
PSALM 3:5

AUGUST

11

How good the Word of God is.

For whatever God says to us is full of living power.

The Bible is useful to teach us what is true, to make us realize what is wrong in our lives. It helps us do what is right.

Happy are all who hear the Word of God and put it into practice.

HEBREWS 6:5   HEBREWS 4:12
2 TIMOTHY 3:16   LUKE 11:28

Nicole Galanos, age 6½

God will help us be true to what we say.

The Lord has commanded that when anyone makes a promise to the Lord, either to do something or to quit doing something, that promise must not be broken.

Trust the Lord to help you do it and he will.

2 CORINTHIANS 2:4   NUMBERS 30:1   PSALM 37:5

Tell the truth.

Truth stands the test of time. Lies are soon found out. A good man is known by his truthfulness.

Never forget to be truthful and kind. For unless you are honest in small matters, you won't be in large ones. If you cheat even a little, you won't be honest with greater duties.

ZECHARIAH 8:16   PROVERBS 12:19, 17
PROVERBS 3:3   LUKE 16:10

Todd Hoskins, age 9

You must not steal.

Remember this—the wrong desires that come into your life aren't anything new and different. Many others have faced the same problems before you. And no temptation is too hard to resist.

Ask the Lord Jesus Christ to help you live as you should.

LEVITICUS 19:11
1 CORINTHIANS 10:13
ROMANS 13:14

Timmy Botts, age 36

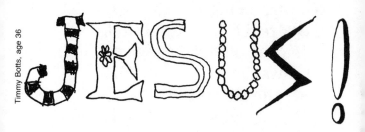

Jesus!

He does not fight or shout.
He does not raise his voice.
He does not crush the weak,
Or snuff out the smallest hope.
   Be full of love for others,
following the example of Jesus
who loved you.

MATTHEW 12:19, 20   EPHESIANS 5:1

AUGUST

16 **Behave like God's very own children.**

Love comes from God and those who are loving and kind show that they are the children of God.

If a person isn't loving and kind, it shows that he doesn't know God—for God is love.

Do only what is good and right and true.

ROMANS 8:15   1 JOHN 4:7, 8   EPHESIANS 5:9

Love overlooks insults.

Don't repay evil for evil. Don't snap
back at those who say unkind
things about you. Instead, pray for
God's help for them. For we are to
be kind to others. God will bless us
for it.

Keep control of your tongue.

PROVERBS 10:12   1 PETER 3:9, 10

Don't grumble about each other.

In everything you do, stay away from complaining and arguing.

When a man is gloomy, everything seems to go wrong. When he is cheerful, everything seems right. A cheerful heart does good like medicine.

JAMES 5:9   PHILIPPIANS 2:14
PROVERBS 15:15   PROVERBS 17:22

Gossip separates the best of friends.

If you want a happy, good life, keep control of your tongue. Guard your lips from telling lies.

Turn away from evil and do good. Try to live in peace even if you must run after it to catch and hold it!

PROVERBS 16:28   1 PETER 3:10, 11

Work happily together.

Don't try to act big.

Don't quarrel with anyone. Be at peace with everyone, just as much as possible.

Be good and true in everything you do so that all can approve your behavior.

Ask the Lord Jesus Christ to help you live as you should.

ROMANS 12:16, 18   ROMANS 13:12, 13, 14

Whatever anyone does to another shall be done to him.

Treat others as you want them to treat you. Don't say, "Now I can pay him back for all his meanness to me!"

Go easy on others. Then they will do the same for you.

LEVITICUS 24:20   LUKE 6:31
PROVERBS 24:29   LUKE 6:37

AUGUST

22

Be patient in trouble.

Take your share of suffering as a good soldier of Jesus Christ.

All that happens to us is working for our good if we love God and are fitting into his plans. For when the way is rough, your patience has a chance to grow.

ROMANS 12:12   2 TIMOTHY 2:1
ROMANS 8:28   JAMES 1:3

Unhappiness comes to the wicked.

But love surrounds those who trust in the Lord.

The hopes of evil men never come true. Wickedness never brings real success. Only the godly have that.

PSALM 32:10   PROVERBS 10:28   PROVERBS 12:3

What is causing the quarrels and fights among you?

Ahab went back angry. He refused to eat and went to bed with his face to the wall.

If you are angry, don't sin by nursing your grudge. Don't let the sun go down while you are still angry—get over it quickly.

JAMES 4:1   1 KINGS 21:4   EPHESIANS 4:26

The Lord is fair in everything he does.

He will give each one whatever his deeds deserve.

He will give eternal life to those who patiently do the will of God.

He will terribly punish those who fight against the truth of God and walk in evil ways.

PSALM 145:17   ROMANS 2:6, 7, 8

Every wrong is a sin.

All have gone wrong. But if we confess our sins to God, he can be depended on to forgive us and to cleanse us from every wrong.

And it is perfectly proper for God to do this for us because Christ died to wash away our sins.

1 JOHN 5:17   ROMANS 3:12   1 JOHN 1:9

God loved the world.

God showed how much he loved us by sending his only Son into this wicked world to bring to us eternal life through his death.

Anyone who believes in him shall have eternal life.

There is salvation in no one else!

JOHN 3:16   1 JOHN 4:9   JOHN 3:16   ACTS 4:12

Jeremy Botts, age 9

Joel Kubin, age 9

Pray about everything.

Pray morning, noon, and night.
God will hear and answer.

Go away by yourself, all alone,
and shut the door behind you. Pray
to your Father secretly, and your
Father, who knows your secrets,
will reward you.

God is able to do far more than
we would ever dare to ask or even
dream of.

PHILIPPIANS 4:6   PSALM 55:17
MATTHEW 6:6   EPHESIANS 3:20

My best friend has turned against me.

But God is my helper. He is a friend of mine! The Lord stands beside me like a great warrior.

If my father and mother should leave me, God would welcome and comfort me.

PSALM 41:9   PSALM 54:4
JEREMIAH 20:11   PSALM 27:10

Does God realize what is going on?

The Lord is watching everywhere. The Lord looks down upon mankind from heaven where he lives.

Nothing can be hidden from him to whom we must explain all that we have done.

PSALM 73:11   PROVERBS 15:3
PSALM 33:13   HEBREWS 4:13

Problems are good for us.

All that happens to us is working
for our good if we love God and are
fitting into his plans.

God himself is caring for you. He
is your defender. He protects you
day and night. He keeps his eye
upon you as you come and go and
always guards you.

ROMANS 5:3   ROMANS 8:28   PSALM 121:5, 6, 8

The eyes of the Lord are watching all who live good lives.

He gives attention when they cry to him.

Yes, the Lord hears the good man when he calls to him for help, and saves him out of all his troubles.

The Lord is close to those whose hearts are breaking. He saves those who are sorry for their sins.

PSALM 34:15, 17, 18

I am sorry for what I have done.

When I want to do good, I don't. When I try not to do wrong, I do it anyway. Don't keep looking at my sins.

Lord, I need your help, especially in my own home, where I long to act as I should.

I will trust him to help me and he will.

PSALM 38:18   ROMANS 7:19
PSALM 51:9   PSALM 101:2   PSALM 37:5

Only a fool would say to himself, "There is no God."

And why does he say it? Because of his wicked heart.

Anyone who talks like that is evil and cannot really be a good person at all.

Since earliest times men have seen the earth and sky and all God made, and have known that he is.

PSALM 53:1 PSALM 14:1 ROMANS 1:20

God alone has all wisdom.

World events are under his control. He removes kings and sets others on their thrones. He gives wise men their wisdom and teachers their knowledge.

He shares mysteries beyond man's understanding. He knows all hidden things.

DANIEL 2:20, 21, 22

God knows what is happening.

O Lord, you know everything about me. You know when I sit or stand. You know my every thought. Every moment you know where I am. You know what I am going to say before I even say it. You know everything.

JOB 23:10   PSALM 139:1, 2, 3, 4

Diana Jeude, age 8

Lord, how you have helped me!

I have depended upon you since birth. You have always been my God.

You are close beside me, guarding, guiding all the way. Your goodness and unfailing kindness shall be with me all of my life.

PSALM 22:9, 11   PSALM 23:4, 6

The needs of the needy shall not be ignored forever.

Lord, you know the hopes of humble people. Surely you will hear their cries and comfort their hearts by helping them.

The Lord replies, "I will arise and defend the poor, the needy. I will rescue them as they have longed for me to do."

PSALM 9:18   PSALM 10:17   PSALM 12:5

**Let
everything
he has
made
give praise
to God.**

For he spoke and they came into being.

Let the mountains and hills, the fruit trees and cedars, the wild animals and cattle, the snakes and birds, all praise the Lord together.

PSALM 148:5, 9, 10, 13

9

A person who calls himself a Christian should not be doing things that are wrong.

God wants us to live good, God-fearing lives day after day.

Try hard to live without sinning. Be at peace with everyone so that God will be pleased with you.

Turn away from everything wrong.

2 TIMOTHY 2:19   TITUS 2:12   2 PETER 3:14
2 CORINTHIANS 7:1

A blow to the nose causes bleeding. So anger causes quarrels.

Don't be quick-tempered. That is being a fool. A soft answer turns away anger.

Stop being mean, bad-tempered, and angry. Quarreling, unkind words, and dislike of others should have no place in your lives.

It is hard to stop a quarrel once it starts, so don't let it begin.

PROVERBS 30:33   ECCLESIASTES 7:9
PROVERBS 15:1   EPHESIANS 4:31
PROVERBS 17:14

Obey your parents. This is the right thing to do.

God has placed them in authority over you.

For their advice is a beam of light directed into the dark corners of your mind to warn you of danger and to give you a good life.

EPHESIANS 6:1   PROVERBS 6:23

Finishing is better than starting.

Work hard and become a leader. Be lazy and never succeed.

Throw yourself into your tasks so that everyone may notice your improvement and progress.

You have a wonderful future ahead of you.

ECCLESIASTES 7:8   PROVERBS 12:24
1 TIMOTHY 4:15   PROVERBS 23:18

Kristen Hamaker, age 7

SEPTEMBER

13

Be full of love for others, following the example of Christ.

Jesus was very fond of Martha, Mary, and Lazarus. He loved his disciples. How full of love and kindness our Lord Jesus was.

Those who are loving and kind show that they are children of God.

EPHESIANS 5:2   JOHN 11:5   JOHN 13:1
2 CORINTHIANS 8:9   1 JOHN 4:7

Love is never jealous.

When you are jealous of one another and divide up into quarreling groups, doesn't that prove you are still babies, wanting your own way?

That isn't the way Christ taught you. Instead, be kind to each other.

1 CORINTHIANS 13:4   1 CORINTHIANS 3:3
EPHESIANS 4:20, 32

You shall not use the name of Jehovah your God disrespectfully.

His joy is in those who reverence him, those who expect him to be loving and kind.

He is like a father to us, tender and understanding to those who honor him.

Respect for God gives life, happiness, and protection from harm.

EXODUS 20:7   PSALM 147:11   PSALM 103:13
PROVERBS 19:23

16

Choose the best.

If you belong to the Lord, reverence him. For everyone who does this has everything he needs.

Even strong young lions sometimes go hungry, but those of us who honor the Lord will never lack any good thing.

PSALM 25:12
PSALM 34:9, 10

Heather Secker, age 6

The free gift of God is eternal life through Jesus Christ our Lord.

Christ became a human being and lived here on earth. He became a man so that he could take away our sins. He died to make us right with God.

We are saved by faith in Christ and not by the good things we do.

ROMANS 6:23   JOHN 1:14   1 JOHN 3:5
ROMANS 4:25   ROMANS 3:28

18

What must I do to be saved?

If you tell others with your own mouth that Jesus Christ is your Lord, and believe in your own heart that God has raised him from the dead, you will be saved.

If you believe that Jesus is the Christ—that he is God's Son and your Savior—then you are a child of God.

ACTS 16:30   ROMANS 10:9   1 JOHN 5:1

Our heavenly Father allows us to be called his children.

To all who receive him, he gives the right to become children of God.

His plan has always been to adopt us into his own family. And so we should behave like God's very own children.

1 JOHN 3:1   JOHN 1:12   EPHESIANS 1:5
ROMANS 8:15

Be careful how you act.

Don't think only of yourself. Try to think of the other fellow, too, and what is best for him. Ask the Lord Jesus Christ to help you live as you should.

Christ didn't please himself. Though he was God, he did not demand and cling to his rights as God.

EPHESIANS 5:15   1 CORINTHIANS 10:24
ROMANS 13:14   ROMANS 15:3   PHILIPPIANS 2:6

You have a new life.

God has saved for his children the priceless gift of eternal life. It is kept in heaven for you.

It was not passed on to you from your parents, for the life they gave you will fade away. This new one will last forever.

1 PETER 1:23, 4, 23

The world is not our home.

God is creating new heavens and a new earth—so wonderful that no one will even think about the old ones anymore.

We are looking forward to God's promise of new heavens and a new earth, where there will be only goodness.

HEBREWS 13:14   ISAIAH 65:17   2 PETER 3:13

You may worship no other God.

Worship only the Lord God. Obey only him.

Obey him gladly. Come before him, singing with joy.

Try to realize what this means. The Lord is God! He made us.

EXODUS 20:3   MATTHEW 4:10   PSALM 100:1, 2, 3

Thank the Lord for all the things he does.

Jehovah is kind and merciful, slow to get angry, full of love. He is good to everyone.

The Lord is fair in everything he does, and full of kindness. He protects all those who love him.

PSALM 105:1   PSALM 145:8, 9, 17, 20

The Lord looks down upon mankind from heaven where he lives.

He has made our hearts and closely watches everything we do.

With a breath he can scatter the plans of all the nations who don't obey him. His own plan stands forever.

We depend upon the Lord alone to save us. Only he can help us. He protects us like a shield.

PSALM 33:13, 14, 15, 10, 11, 20

The Lord lives on forever.

He sits upon his throne to judge the nations of the world. All who are sad may come to him. He is a comfort for them in their times of trouble.

All those who know your mercy, Lord, will count on you for help. For you have never yet turned away from those who trust in you.

PSALM 8:7, 8, 9, 10

Food and drink ... even this pleasure is from the hand of God.

He sends rain upon the mountains
and fills the earth with fruit.

The tender grass grows up at his
command to feed the cattle.

There are fruit trees, vegetables,
and grain for man to grow.

He gives food to every living
thing. Give thanks to the God of
heaven.

ECCLESIASTES 2:24, 25   PSALM 104:13, 14
PSALM 136:25, 26

"Who makes mouths?" Jehovah asked.

"Isn't it I, the Lord?"
"Who makes a man so that he can speak or not speak, see or not see, hear or not hear?"
If you have good eyesight and good hearing, thank God who gave them to you.

EXODUS 2:11   PROVERBS 20:12

Practice tenderhearted mercy and kindness to others.

David met Jonathan, the king's son, and there was an immediate bond of love between them. Jonathan gave him his robe, sword, bow, and belt. For he loved him as much as he loved himself.

You can have real love for everyone.

COLOSSIANS 3:12   1 SAMUEL 18:1, 2, 3, 4
1 SAMUEL 20:17   1 PETER 1:22

Be interested in others and in what they are doing.

Don't think only of yourself. Let everyone see that you are unselfish and polite in all you do.

It is good when you truly obey our Lord's command.

PHILIPPIANS 2:4   1 CORINTHIANS 10:24
PHILIPPIANS 4:5   JAMES 2:8

Honor God in your youth.

For his mercy toward those who fear and honor him is as great as the height of the heavens above the earth.

To do right honors God.

To help the poor is to honor God.

ECCLESIASTES 12:1   PSALM 103:11
PROVERBS 14:2, 31

Remember to help the poor.

The rich and the poor are alike before the Lord who made them all.

To help the poor is to honor God. God blesses those who are kind to the poor. He helps them out of their troubles.

FOR YOU

GALATIANS 2:10 PROVERBS 22:2
PROVERBS 14:31 PSALM 41:1

OCTOBER

3

Don't just think about your own business.

Try to think of the other fellow, and what is best for him. We cannot just go ahead and please ourselves. We must be considerate of the doubts and fears of others.

Be interested in others, and in what they are doing.

PHILIPPIANS 2:4   1 CORINTHIANS 10:24
ROMANS 15:2   PHILIPPIANS 2:4

If you give, you will get!

It isn't important how much you have to give. God wants you to give what you have, not what you haven't.

If you give even a cup of cold water to a little child, you will surely be rewarded.

If you have extra food, give it away to those who are hungry.

LUKE 6:38   2 CORINTHIANS 8:12
MATTHEW 10:42   LUKE 3:10

Observe the Sabbath as a holy day.

This is the day the Lord has made. Let us not ignore our church meetings as some people do.

Sing his praises with music from the harp and lute and lyre.

EXODUS 20:8   PSALM 118:24   HEBREWS 10:25
PSALM 92:3

Come, kneel before the Lord our Maker.

He is our God. We are his sheep, and he is our Shepherd. Oh, that you would hear him calling you today and come to him.

Oh, come, let us sing to the Lord. Come before him with thankful hearts. Let us sing him psalms of praise. For the Lord is a great God.

PSALM 95:6, 1, 2, 3

How much God loves us.

God showed how much he loved us by sending his only Son into this wicked world to bring to us eternal life.

You must love him with all your heart, soul, and might.

When you think of what he has done for you, is this too much to ask?

1 JOHN 4:16   1 JOHN 4:9   DEUTERONOMY 6:5
ROMANS 12:1

Jesus said, "If you love me, obey me."

Loving God means doing what he tells you to do. And really, that isn't hard at all.

He has told you what he wants, and this is all it is: to be fair and just and merciful, and to walk humbly with your God.

JOHN 14:15   1 JOHN 5:3   MICAH 6:8

Do what is good and right and true.

Stop lying to each other. Tell the truth. When we lie to each other we are hurting ourselves.

If you are angry, don't sin by nursing your grudge. Get over it quickly.

If anyone is stealing, he must stop it.

Don't use bad language. Say only what is good and helpful to those you are talking to.

EPHESIANS 5:9   EPHESIANS 4:25, 26, 28, 29

Be happy.

When a man is gloomy, everything seems to go wrong. When he is cheerful, everything seems right!

A cheerful heart does good like medicine.

Be like one big happy family.

2 CORINTHIANS 13:11   PROVERBS 15:15
PROVERBS 17:22   1 PETER 3:8

11

A true friend is always loyal.

If you love someone you will be loyal to him no matter what the cost. You will always believe in him, always expect the best of him, and always stand your ground in defending him.

When others are happy be happy with them. If they are sad, share their sorrow.

PROVERBS 17:17   1 CORINTHIANS 13:7
ROMANS 12:15

Soren Johnson, age 9

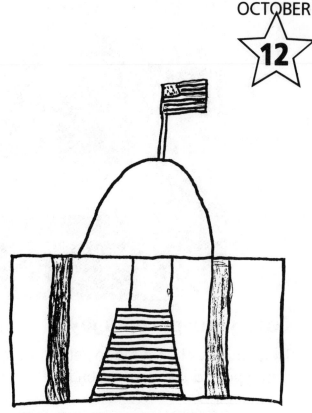

Pray much for others.

Pray for kings and all others who are in authority over us, so that we can live in peace and quietness.

This is good and pleases God our Savior.

1 TIMOTHY 2:1, 2, 3

13

Give your parents joy!

Don't always be trying to get out of doing your duty, even when it's unpleasant.

Let everyone be sure that he is doing his very best. Then he will have the personal satisfaction of work well done. He won't need to compare himself with someone else.

PROVERBS 23:25   ECCLESIASTES 8:2
GALATIANS 6:4

Be kind and good to others.

Because of all God has done for us, let us outdo each other in being helpful and kind to each other and in doing good.

When others are happy, be happy with them. If they are sad, share their sorrow.

Be like one big happy family, full of sympathy toward each other.

PSALM 37:3
HEBREWS 10:24
ROMANS 12:15
1 PETER 3:8

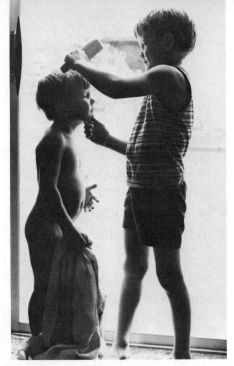

A brother is born to help in time of need.

I was hungry and you fed me.

I was thirsty and you gave me water.

I was naked and you clothed me.

I was sick and in prison and you visited me.

Let us outdo each other in being helpful and kind to each other and in doing good.

PROVERBS 17:17   MATTHEW 25:35, 36
HEBREWS 10:24

Always be doing good, kind things.

Make the most of every chance you have for doing good.

Treat others as you want them to treat you.

Never criticize or it will all come back on you. Go easy on others. Then they will do the same for you.

PHILIPPIANS 1:11   EPHESIANS 5:16
LUKE 6:31, 37

God will use you to help others.

Cheerful givers are the ones God prizes.

Don't think only of yourself. Try to think of the other person and what is best for them.

Learn to do good. Share what you have.

1 TIMOTHY 4:16   2 CORINTHIANS 9:7
1 CORINTHIANS 10:24   ISAIAH 1:17
HEBREWS 13:16

Don't worry about things— food, drink, and clothes.

For you already have life and a body. They are far more important than what to eat and wear!

Look at the birds. They don't worry about what to eat. They don't need to store up food. For your heavenly Father feeds them. And you are far more valuable to him than they are.

MATTHEW 6:25, 26

Kevin Johnson, age 6

Christ became a man so that he could take away our sins.

God showed how much he loved us by sending his only Son into this wicked world to bring to us eternal life.

He died for us so that we can live with him forever.

1 JOHN 3:5   1 JOHN 4:9   1 THESSALONIANS 5:10

Jesus taught in the synagogue and surprised everyone.

He became well known. Great crowds surrounded him to listen to the Word of God. The crowds grew until there were thousands upon thousands.

"He says such wonderful things!" they said. "We've never heard anything like it."

MATTHEW 13:53, 54   LUKE 4:14   LUKE 5:1
LUKE 12:1   JOHN 7:46

Jesus grew both tall and wise, and was loved by God and man.

Christ is far, far above any other king or ruler or dictator or leader.

"How is this possible?" the people exclaimed. "He's just a carpenter's son. How can he be so great?"

Jesus is Lord.

LUKE 2:52   EPHESIANS 1:20, 21
MATTHEW 13:55, 56   PHILIPPIANS 2:10

22

Heather Secker, age 6

Christ has come from heaven and is greater than anyone else.

God raised him up to the heights of heaven and gave him a name which is above every other name. At the name of Jesus every knee shall bow in heaven and earth and under the earth. And every tongue shall confess that Jesus Christ is Lord.

He sits beside God in the place of honor and power.

JOHN 3:31   PHILIPPIANS 2:9, 10, 11
COLOSSIANS 3:1

The Lord sees every heart and understands and knows every thought.

The Lord is watching everywhere and keeps his eye on both the evil and the good. The depths of hell are open to God's knowledge. How much more the hearts of all mankind!

He counts the stars and calls them all by name. How great he is! His power is absolute! His understanding is unlimited.

1 CHRONICLES 28:9   PROVERBS 15:3, 11
PSALM 147:4, 5

The Lord rules from heaven.

That man is a fool who says to himself, "There is no God!" Anyone who talks like that is evil and cannot really be a good person at all.

The Lord closely watches everything that happens here on earth. He puts the righteous and the wicked to the test.

God is a judge who is perfectly fair.

PSALM 11:4   PSALM 14:1   PSALM 11:4, 5
PSALM 7:11

All are equal before the Lord.

For he doesn't care how great a man may be, and doesn't pay any more attention to the rich than the poor. He made them all.

One's nationality or race or education or social position is unimportant. Such things mean nothing. Whether a person has Christ is what matters.

NUMBERS 15:16   JOB 34:19   COLOSSIANS 3:11

You can sleep without fear.

You don't need to be afraid of the dark any more, nor fear the dangers of the day. For he orders his angels to protect you wherever you go.

You need not be afraid of disaster for the Lord is with you. He protects you.

PROVERBS 3:24   PSALM 91:5, 11
PROVERBS 3:25, 26

Christ will not leave you.

If a man has a hundred sheep, and one wanders away and is lost, what will he do? Won't he leave the ninety-nine others and go out into the hills to search for the lost one? And if he finds it, he will rejoice over it more than over the ninety-nine others safe at home.

How much more valuable is a person than a sheep!

MATTHEW 18:12, 13
JOHN 14:18
MATTHEW 12:12

We are his sheep and he is our Shepherd.

What pity Jesus felt for the crowds that came, because their problems were so great and they didn't know what to do or where to go for help. They were like sheep without a shepherd.

He taught them many things they needed to know. And he became their Savior.

PSALM 95:7   MATTHEW 9:36   MARK 6:34
ISAIAH 63:8

Jesus told him, "I am the Way—yes, and the Truth and the Life.

I will not leave you alone in the storm. I will come to you.

I am leaving you with a gift— peace of mind and heart. And the peace I give isn't fragile like the peace the world gives. So don't be troubled or afraid. Live within my love.

JOHN 14:6, 18, 27   JOHN 15:9

Jesus went around doing good.

Once when some mothers were bringing their children to Jesus to bless them, the disciples shooed them away, telling them not to bother him.

But when Jesus saw what was happening he said to them, "Let the children come to me, for the Kingdom of God belongs to such as they."

Children are a gift from God. They are his reward.

ACTS 10:38   MARK 10:13, 14   PSALM 127:3

OCTOBER

31

We are all children of God.

God is like a father to us, tender and understanding.

His unchanging plan has always been to adopt us into his own family by sending Jesus Christ to die for us.

He allows us to be called his children—think of it—and we really are!

GALATIANS 3:26   PSALM 103:13   EPHESIANS 1:5
1 JOHN 3:1

God loves us.

God showed how much he loved us by sending Jesus into this wicked world.

Jesus never sinned. He never told a lie. He never answered back when insulted. He did not threaten to get even. He died a criminal's death on a cross.

Christ died to wash away our sins.

ROMANS 5:5   1 JOHN 4:9   1 PETER 2:22, 23
PHILIPPIANS 2:8   1 JOHN 1:9

Jesus knew mankind to the core.

Jesus knew what they were thinking and asked them, "Why are you thinking such evil thoughts?"

Jesus surprised everyone with his wisdom and his miracles.

O Lord, you know everything about me. You know when I sit or stand. When far away you know my every thought.

JOHN 2:24   MATTHEW 9:4   MATTHEW 13:54
PSALM 139:1, 2

I am the Lord.
I do not change.

Jesus Christ is the same
yesterday, today, and
forever.
The living, unchanging God.
He delivers his people,
keeping them from harm.
He does great miracles
in heaven and earth.

MALACHI 3:6   HEBREWS 13:8
DANIEL 6:26, 27

NOVEMBER

With God everything is possible.

4

All of the people of the earth are nothing when compared to him. He does whatever he thinks best among the hosts of heaven, as well as here among the people of earth. No one can stop him or question him, saying, "What do you mean by doing these things?"

MARK 10:27   DANIEL 4:35

"Who is this that even the winds and the sea obey him?"

He quiets the raging oceans and all the world's noise. He calms the storm and stills the waves.

Who else but God? Who else holds the wind in his fists and wraps up the oceans in his coat?

Who but God has created the world?

MATTHEW 8:27   PSALM 65:7   PSALM 107:29
PROVERBS 30:4

Is anything too hard for God?

God is in the heavens and does as he wishes. He does whatever pleases him all over heaven and earth, and in the deepest seas.

World events are under his control. He removes kings and sets others on their thrones. No other God can do what this one does.

DANIEL 3:29 DANIEL 2:2
GENESIS 18:14
PSALM 135:6
PSALM 115:3

How can we describe God?

Who else has held the oceans in his hands and measured off the heavens with his ruler?

Who else knows the weight of all the earth and weighs the mountains and the hills?

Has he ever needed anyone's advice? Did he need instruction as to what is right and best?

With what can we compare him?

PSALM 40:18, 12, 14, 18

We feel God's presence in the thunder.

The God of glory thunders through the skies. So powerful is his voice, so full of majesty.

By his fantastic powers in nature he punishes or blesses his people.

We cannot understand the greatness of his power.

JOB 36:33   PSALM 29:3, 4   JOB 36:31   JOB 37:5

James Claud, age 6

We were doomed by our sins.

God declares us not guilty of wronging him if we trust in Jesus Christ.

For God sent Christ Jesus to take the punishment for our sins.

We can all be saved by coming to Christ.

EPHESIANS 2:5   ROMANS 3:24, 25, 22

I Pray to god.

Believe on the Lord Jesus and you will be saved.

If you believe that Jesus is the Christ—that he is God's Son and your Savior—then you are a child of God.

You have been saved through trusting Christ.

John Miller, age 8

ACTS 16:31   1 JOHN 5:1   EPHESIANS 2:8

11

Jesus Christ is far greater than any king in all the earth.

He told his disciples, "I have been given all power in heaven and earth."

He has come from heaven and is greater than anyone else.

At the name of Jesus every knee shall bow in heaven and on earth and under the earth, and every tongue shall confess that Jesus Christ is Lord.

REVELATION 1:5   MATTHEW 28:18   JOHN 3:31
PHILIPPIANS 2:10, 11

Christ has always been alive.

Before anything else was, there was Christ. He created everything there is. He was before all else began and it is his power that holds everything together. He controls the universe by the mighty power of his command. He is the one who died to cleanse us and clear our record of all sin.

JOHN 1:2   JOHN 1:1, 3   COLOSSIANS 1:17
HEBREWS 1:3

Jesus lives forever.

In ages past you laid the foundations of the earth, and made the heavens with your hands. They shall die, but you go on forever.

You never grow old. You are forever.

Jesus Christ is the same yesterday, today, and forever.

HEBREWS 7:24   PSALM 102:25, 26, 27
HEBREWS 13:8

I will be your God.

I made you and I will care for you. I will carry you along and be your Savior.

I will keep the promise I made to you when you were young. I will be your God through all your lifetime, yes, even when your hair is white with age.

ISAIAH 46:4   EZEKIEL 16:60   ISAIAH 46:4

Douglas Scott, age 7

It will all be yours.

God has kept for his children the priceless gift of eternal life. It is kept in heaven for you, beyond the reach of change and growing old.

And God will make sure that you get there safely to receive it, because you are trusting him.

1 PETER 1:5, 4, 5

Love the Lord your God with all your heart, soul, and mind.

Be delighted with the Lord. Then he will give you all your heart's desires.

All that happens to us is working for our good if we love God and are fitting into his plans.

If we love God, we will do whatever he tells us to.

MATTHEW 22:37   PSALM 37:4   ROMANS 8:28
2 JOHN 6

Love your neighbor as much as you love yourself.

All Ten Commandments are wrapped up in this one—to love your neighbor as you love yourself.

Love does no wrong to anyone. That's why it fully satisfies all that God requires. It is the only law you need.

MATTHEW 22:39   ROMANS 13:9, 10

Don't complain about each other.

In everything you do, stay away from complaining and arguing.

Be glad for all God is planning for you. Always be thankful. And whatever you do, do it with kindness and love.

JAMES 5:9   PHILIPPIANS 2:14   ROMANS 12:12
1 THESSALONIANS 5:18   1 CORINTHIANS 16:14

19

Do not be proud.

Don't try to act big. Don't think you know it all. Although being a know-it-all makes us feel important, what is really needed is love.

Love is never boastful or proud.

ROMANS 11:20   ROMANS 12:16
1 CORINTHIANS 8:1   1 CORINTHIANS 13:4

Tell the truth.

Stop lying to each other.
When we lie
to each other
we are hurting
ourselves.

Telling lies
about someone
is as harmful
as hitting him
with an axe,
or wounding him
with a sword,
or shooting him
with a sharp arrow.

EPHESIANS 4:25   PROVERBS 25:18

Jeremy Botts, age 9

The Lord hates cheating and delights in honesty.

Some men enjoy cheating, but the cake they get by cheating will turn to gravel in their mouths.

Better to be poor and honest than rich and a cheater. For God carefully watches the goings on of all mankind. He sees them all.

PROVERBS 11:1   PROVERBS 20:17
PROVERBS 28:6   JOB 34:21

**You children
must always obey
your fathers and mothers,
for that pleases the Lord.**

Don't be like a senseless horse or
mule that has to have a bit in its
mouth to keep it in line.

Anyone willing to be
corrected is on the
pathway to life.
Anyone refusing
has lost his chance.

COLOSSIANS 3:20   PSALM 32:9   PROVERBS 10:17

NOVEMBER

23

To learn, you must want to be taught.

Only fools refuse to be taught. Listen to your father and mother. What you learn from them will do you good. It will gain you many honors.

Students are wise who master what their teachers tell them. Throw yourself into your tasks.

PROVERBS 12:1   PROVERBS 1:8, 9
ECCLESIASTES 12:11   1 TIMOTHY 4:15

God will give you leaders after his own heart.

Honor the officers of your church who work hard among you and warn you against all that is wrong. Think highly of them and give them your love. Think of all the good that has come from their lives.

Try to trust the Lord as they do.

JEREMIAH 3:15   1 THESSALONIANS 5:12, 13
HEBREWS 13:7

Don't recite the same prayer over and over.

Tell God your needs. He will give them to you if you give him first place in your life and live as he wants you to.

Pray about everything. And don't forget to thank him for his answers.

MATTHEW 6:7   PHILIPPIANS 4:6   MATTHEW 6:33
PHILIPPIANS 4:6

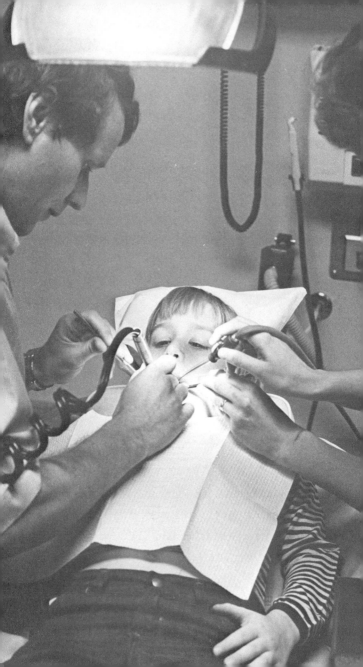

Trust God in your times of trouble.

The king broke into tears, and went up to his room crying as he went.

The good man does not escape all troubles—he has them too. But the Lord helps him in each and every one.

He is like a father to us.

PSALM 50:15   2 SAMUEL 18:33   PSALM 34:19
PSALM 103:13

27

You have always been my God.

I have depended upon you since birth.

All those who know your mercy, Lord, will count on you for help. For you have never yet left those who trust in you.

You do such wonderful things. You planned them long ago. Your love and kindness are forever.

PSALM 22:10   PSALM 9:10   ISAIAH 25:1
PSALM 89:2

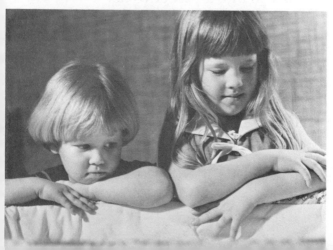

Every word of God proves true.

Remember what Christ taught and let his words enrich your lives and make you wise.

Some people may deny these things, but they are the true teachings of the Lord Jesus Christ. They are the starting point for a godly life.

God's words will always prove true and right no matter who questions them.

PROVERBS 30:5   COLOSSIANS 3:16
1 TIMOTHY 6:3   ROMANS 3:4

The Word of the Lord will last forever.

All who listen to my instructions and follow them are wise, like a man who builds his house on solid rock. Though the rain comes down, and the floods rise, and the storm winds beat against his house, it won't fall, for it is built on rock.

1 PETER 1:25   MATTHEW 7:24, 25

Heaven and earth will disappear, but God's words remain forever.

Search the Book of the Lord and see all that he will do. Not one detail will he miss, for the Lord has said it. His Spirit will make it all come true.

The grass withers, the flowers fade, but the Word of our God shall stand forever.

MATTHEW 24:35   ISAIAH 34:16   ISAIAH 40:8

1

Let everything he has made give praise to God.

PSALM 148:5, 9, 11, 12, 13

For he spoke and they came into being.

Let the kings and all the people, with their rulers and their judges, young men and women, old men and children, all praise the Lord together. For he alone is worthy.

God loves goodness.

He loves whatever is just and good.

Our God will make you the kind of children he wants to have. He will make you as good as you wish you could be!

God is more pleased when we are just and fair than when we give him gifts.

PSALM 11:7   PSALM 33:5   2 THESSALONIANS 1:11
PROVERBS 21:3

The good person's life is full of light.

No man has ever seen, heard, or even imagined what wonderful things God has ready for those who love the Lord.

The Lord will give you lots of good things.

You will live in joy and peace. The mountains and hills, the trees of the field—all the world around you—will rejoice.

PROVERBS 13:9   1 CORINTHIANS 2:9
DEUTERONOMY 28:11   ISAIAH 55:12

You have a wonderful future ahead of you!

Be delighted with the Lord. Then he will give you all your heart's desires. Commit everything you do to the Lord. Trust him to help you do it and he will.

He never forgets his promises.

PROVERBS 23:17   PSALM 37:4, 5   PSALM 111:5

The Lord God is for me!

Because the Lord God helps me, I will not be afraid.

I can say without any doubt or fear, "The Lord is my Helper."

My help is from Jehovah who made the mountains.

ISAIAH 50:9
ISAIAH 50:7
HEBREWS 13:6
PSALM 121:2

**O Lord our God,
the glory of your name
fills all the earth
and overflows the heavens.**

The heavens are a marvelous
display of your work. Day and
night they keep on telling about
God. Without a sound or word,
silent in the skies, their message
reaches out to all the world.

PSALM 8:1   PSALM 19:1, 2, 3, 4

DECEMBER

7

O Lord,
what a variety
you have made!

The ostrich passes
the fastest horse
with its rider.
The horse paws
the earth and
rejoices in his
strength.
The eagle lives upon the
cliffs, making her home
in your mountain.
God made all sorts of
wild animals and cattle
and reptiles. PSALM 104:24

JOB 39:13, 18, 19, 21, 27, 28   GENESIS 1:25

Who can be compared with God?

For all the animals of field and forest are his. The cattle on a thousand hills. And all the birds upon the mountains.

Who else but God goes back and forth to heaven? Who else holds the wind in his fists, and wraps up the oceans in his coat?

Who but God has created the world? If there is any other, what is his name?

PSALM 113:5   PSALM 50:10   PROVERBS 30:4

You shall not make yourselves any idols.

There is only one God, the Father, who created all things and made us to be his own.

Dear children, keep away from anything that might take God's place in your hearts.

EXODUS 20:4   1 CORINTHIANS 8:6   1 JOHN 5:21

Remember what Christ taught.

These laws are not just words. Through obeying them you will live a long, happy life.

Guard my words as the best thing you have. Write them down, and also keep them deep within your heart.

COLOSSIANS 3:16   DEUTERONOMY 32:46
PROVERBS 7:2, 3

The word of the Lord is true.

The whole Bible was given to us by God and is useful to teach us what is true and to make us realize what is wrong in our lives. It straightens us out and helps us do what is right.

2 SAMUEL 22:31   2 TIMOTHY 3:16

DECEMBER 12

You must keep all of my commandments, for I am the Lord.

Never forget the things I've taught you. If you want a long and satisfying life, closely follow my instructions.

I will give you a long life if you follow me and obey my laws.

Do you want a long, good life? Then watch your tongue. Keep your lips from lying.

LEVITICUS 22:31   PROVERBS 3:1   1 KINGS 3:14
PSALM 34:12, 13

God protects you day and night.

God is alive! Praise him who is the great rock of protection. He is the God who pays back those who harm me.

The Lord is my fort where I can enter and be safe. He is a mountain where I hide. He is a rock where none can reach me, and a tower of safety. He is my shield.

PSALM 121:6   PSALM 18:46, 47, 2

DECEMBER

14

**Consider
the wonderful
miracles
of God.**

Do you know how God controls all nature and causes the lightning to flash forth from the clouds?

Do you understand the balancing of the clouds with wonderful perfection and skill?

Do you know why you become warm when the south wind is blowing and everything is still?

We cannot comprehend the greatness of his power.

JOB 37:14, 15, 16, 17, 5

15

As long as the earth remains, there will be springtime and harvest, winter and summer.

The earth belongs to God. He sends the snow in all its lovely whiteness, and scatters the frost upon the ground. He calls for warmer weather, and the spring winds blow. He covers the heavens with clouds, sends down the showers, and makes the green grass grow.

He fills your barns with plenty of the finest wheat.

GENESIS 8:22   PSALM 24:1
PSALM 147:16, 18, 8, 14

16

From the south comes the rain. From the north, the cold.

God directs the snow, the showers, and storm to fall upon the earth.

Man's work stops at such a time, so that all men everywhere may see his power. The wild animals hide in the rocks or in their dens.

Do you know how God controls all nature?

JOB 37:9, 6, 7, 8, 15

I know that God can do anything and that no one can stop him.

God is in the heavens, and does as he wishes.

God is almighty and yet does not dislike anyone.

God is all-powerful. Who is a teacher like him?

JOB 42:2   PSALM 115:3   JOB 36:5, 22

Who holds the wind in his fists?

Who else but God?

Who else has held the oceans in his hands and measured off the heavens with his ruler?

Who else knows the weight of all the earth and weighs the mountains and the hills?

Who else but God?

PROVERBS 30:4   ISAIAH 40:12   PROVERBS 30:4

Power belongs to God.

Our God formed the earth by his power and wisdom. By his knowledge he hung the stars in space and stretched out the heavens. It is his voice that echoes in the thunder of the storm clouds. He causes mist to rise upon the earth. He sends the lightning and brings the rain. From his treasuries he brings the wind.

PSALM 68:34
JEREMIAH 10:12, 15

Many people can build houses, but only God made everything.

He spoke, and the heavens were formed, and all the galaxies of stars. He made the oceans.

Let everyone in all the world— men, women, and children—fear the Lord and stand in wonder of him.

HEBREWS 3:4 PSALM 33:6, 7, 8

Come, see the wonderful things that our God does.

All the world from east to west will know there is no other God. I am Jehovah and there is no one else. I alone am God. I form the light and make the dark. I send good times and bad.

Let all the world look to me for salvation. For I am God. There is no other.

PSALM 46:8   ISAIAH 45:6, 7, 22

Christ became a human being and lived here on earth.

It was because he did this that God gave him a name which is above every other name. At the name of Jesus every tongue shall confess that Jesus Christ is Lord.

And now Christ is in heaven, sitting next to God the Father, with all the angels and powers of heaven bowing before him and obeying him.

JOHN 1:14   PHILIPPIANS 2:9, 10, 11   1 PETER 3:22

Understand who Christ is.

All that Christ is and does marks him as God.

He controls the universe.

He is the one who died to cleanse us and clear our record of all sin.

His name is far greater than the names and titles of the angels.

EPHESIANS 1:17   HEBREWS 1:3, 4

Everything he does is wonderful!

Be full of love for others, following the example of Christ who loved you.

He never sinned. He never told a lie. He never answered back when insulted. When he suffered he did not threaten to get even. He left his case in the hands of God who always judges fairly.

MARK 7:37   EPHESIANS 5:2   1 PETER 2:22, 23

The Savior has been born tonight in Bethlehem.

Christ became a human being and lived here on earth. But although he made the world, the world didn't recognize him when he came. He was not accepted.

But you know that he became a man so that he could take away our sins.

No one who believes in Christ will ever be disappointed.

LUKE 2:11   JOHN 1:14, 10, 11   1 JOHN 3:5
ROMANS 10:11

DECEMBER
26

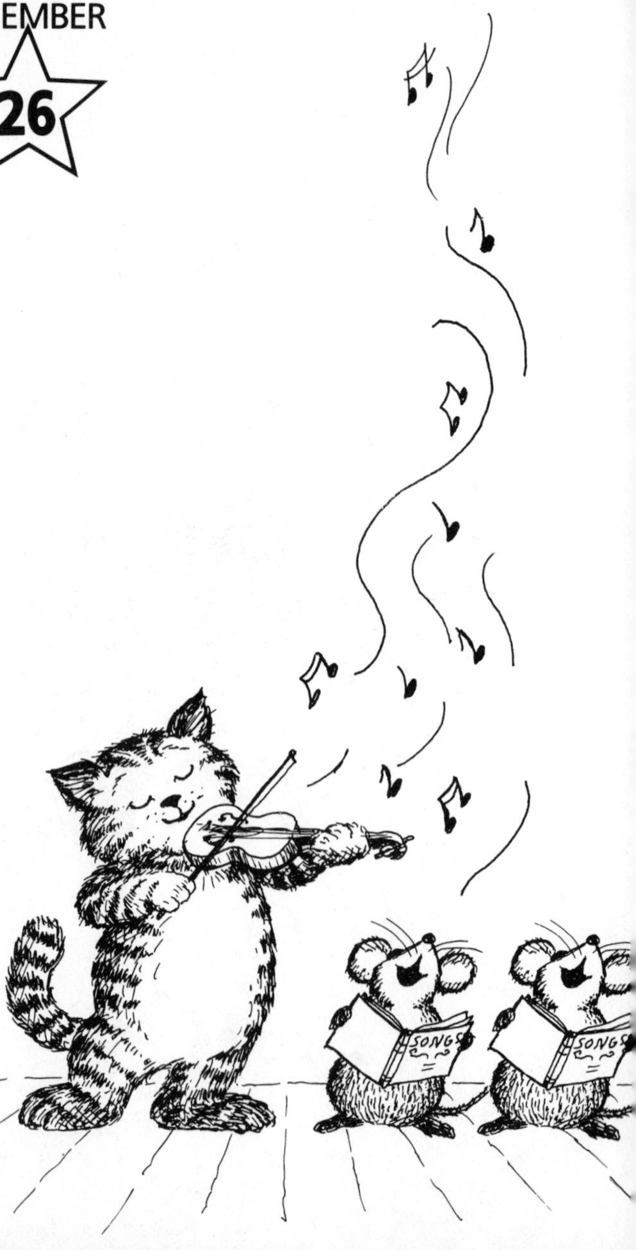

We will write songs to celebrate your mighty acts!

Sing to the Lord, O earth.
Declare each day that he
  is the one who saves!
Show his glory to the nations!
Tell everyone about
  his miracles.
For the Lord is great,
  and should be
  highly praised.

PSALM 21:13   1 CHRONICLES 16:23, 24, 25

Thank you, Lord!

How good you are!

Who can ever list your marvelous miracles? Who can ever praise you half enough? Your love for us continues on forever.

Let all the people say,
"Amen!"
"Praise the Lord!"

PSALM 106:1, 2, 1, 48

Be sure that you do all the Lord has told you to.

Remember what Christ taught.

- Turn from sin, and turn to God.
- Love the Lord your God with all your heart, soul, and mind.
- Honor your father and mother.
- Treat others as you want them to treat you.

COLOSSIANS 4:17   COLOSSIANS 3:16
MATTHEW 4:17   MATTHEW 22:37
MATTHEW 15:4   LUKE 6:31

God will make you the kind of children he wants to have.

God is at work within you, helping you do what he wants. You already know how to please God in your daily living, for you know the commands.

God will make you as good as you wish you could be!

2 THESSALONIANS 1:11   PHILIPPIANS 2:13
1 THESSALONIANS 4:1   2 THESSALONIANS 1:11

Stand silent!

Know that I am God!

I will be honored by every nation in the world!

For at the name of Jesus every knee shall bow in heaven and on earth and under the earth. And every tongue shall confess that Jesus Christ is Lord.

PSALM 46:10   PHILIPPIANS 2:10, 11

**I close with
these last words:**

1. BE HAPPY.

2. GROW IN CHRIST.

3. PAY ATTENTION
to what I have said.

4. *Live in harmony
and peace.*

5. And may the God of love and
peace be with you.

2 CORINTHIANS 13:11

A WONDERful Hooray to:

ARTISTS, LARGE & SMALL

Raechel Anderson: January 2
Christopher Andreoli: January 19
Ben Atkinson: March 27
Kristy Balke: April 13
Jessica Beal: August 3
Dirk Bosgraf: June 9
Jeremy Botts: February 21. April 17. June 1. August 27. November 20.
Katy Botts: January 13
Timmy Botts: August 15
Robin Brumley: March 29
Jennifer Brown: March 2
James Claud: November 9
Amy Cook: January 26
Debby Dvorak: May 3
Mitchell Freeman: January 16. February 29. May 23.
Nicole Galanos: August 12
Katie Gieser: April 29. June 5.
John Goodell: February 6
Roy Green: January 5, 9, 17, 23, 27. February 5, 19, 20, 22, 25. March 1, 6, 15, 18, 24. April 1, 5, 8, 14, 21, 27, 28. May 5, 11, 15, 16, 24, 31. June 7, 14, 25, 28. July 5, 7, 12, 22, 23, 26, 27. August 2, 10, 14, 18, 25. September 2, 9, 10, 18. October 2, 5, 8, 16, 20, 24, 26, 31. November 4, 11, 17, 21, 22, 28, 30. December 2, 9, 14, 19, 25, 29.

Kristen Hamaker: September 12
Corbin Hillam: March 12, 13, 20, 23. April 22, 23. May 9, 10, 22, 25. June 11. July 20, 21. August 20, 21. September 14. October 11. November 2, 8, 29. December 12, 13.
Toni Horman: January 7. February 3, 7, 19, 20. March 3, 25, 26. April 19. May 1, 19. June 20. July 4, 9, 10, 13, 14. August 5, 6. September 8, 28. October 5, 27. November 5, 6. December 16, 17, 26.
Leslie Horton: May 18
Todd Hoskins: January 15. June 10. August 13.
Chris Imhoff: January 29
Diana Jeude: April 18. September 6.
Kevin Johnson: October 19
Soren Johnson: October 12
Chelsea Kellow: January 1
Beth Kenney: February 15
Joel Kubin: June 30. August 28.
Kristy Kunard: July 30
Jennifer Miller: February 28
John Miller: March 4. November 10. December 28.
Heather Oleari: June 21
Andy Oury: June 17
Kendra Pardue: April 16
Colleen Rehr: July 15, 16
Rubberstampede: January 24.

April 25. July 1, 28. September 3, 21. October 7.

Jon Sanchez: February 2

Steve Schick: January 8

Douglas Scott: November 15

Heather Secker: September 16. October 18, 22.

Emily Showalter: February 8. April 7.

Fawnya Slinger: November 24

Ami Sparkman: January 4

Doran Stambaugh: May 21

Cassandra VanDerMolen: August 4

Loribeth VanDerMolen: April 24

Kevin VanderKlay: March 8

Holly Weidenaar: February 27. December 15.

Aimee Wheeler: February 14

Jason Willcutt: May 14

Christa Zapfe: March 17

PICTURE TAKERS

Hildegard Adler: September 19

Animals/Animals: February 12. March 30. April 6, 12. July 2, 29. September 1, 30. October 9. November 18.

Marja Bergen: March 9, 21. May 26.

Stu Berger: March 7

Paul Brackley: front and back cover

Paul Buddle: January 6, 30. February 26. March 5. April 3, 11. May 4, 6. June 13. September 4. November 27.

Jerry Bushey/Trinity Photos: August 6

Bob Combs/Free Vision: January 25, 28. May 28, 30. July 24, 25. August 8, 9. September 7, 22. November 13. December 10.

Hope Cook/Trinity Photos: May 13. August 16.

Jerry Davis/The Resourcery: October 1

Bob Herbert: January 31. May 17.

J.T. Photos: July 6

Wm. Koechling: April 15. June 3, 8. August 11. September 11. October 21.

Robert Maust: March 10, 16, 20. May 20. July 8, 18. August 17, 30. October 10, 25. December 1, 7, 18.

Tom Mcguire: January 22. February 4. October 15.

R. Meier/Trinity Photos: November 26. December 20.

Ron Meyer/White Eyes Design: January 1

Joanne Meldrum: June 6. September 13.

Herb Montgomery: April 10. September 27.

R. Mullin: October 4

Roger W. Neal: June 18, 19. July 11.

Neal Nicolay: December 5

Robert Norris: February 9

Kenneth C. Poertner: July 19

H. Armstrong Roberts: February 24. May 27. December 6.

Robert Settles: July 3

James L. Shaffer: January 10, 11, 18. February 1, 10, 16, 18. March 14. April 26. May 2, 8. June 23, 26. August 22. September 27. October 14. November 23. December 27.

Florence Sharp: April 20. June 27.

Vernon Sigl: December 30

Rick Smolan: June 16. September 20.

Jim Steere: September 23

Dave Swan: March 22. August 24.

Bob Taylor: January 21. March 19. April 30. May 6. August 1, 26. October 13.

Tom Terezakis: August 29

Mary Elenz Tranter: January 20

Andy Watts: November 16

Jim West: December 4

Jim Whitmer: January 3. September 25, 26, 29.

Vera Wulf/Sunrise Photos: January 14. October 28. November 19.

Dan Zamostny: July 31

Living Bible devotional books are available for Grandma, Grandpa, Mom and Dad, brothers, sisters, and all your friends.

WONDER: WHAT A KID SHOULD KNOW. Appeals to children ages 6-8 who are at that "wonder" stage of their lives. Delightful illustrations and photographs. Kivar.

COOL: HOW A KID SHOULD LIVE. Designed for children 8-10 to teach basic principles of Christian living. Heavily illustrated. Kivar.

STRETCH: HOW A KID SHOULD GROW. Daily readings take kids 11-14 through the Bible, book-by-book in a way that captures their interest. Photographs throughout relate the truth to their lives. Kivar.

IN TOUCH. An excellent gift book for teen-agers. Scripture readings are adapted from *Living Light*. Deluxe Graduation and Christmas editions available. Photographs. Kivar and cloth.

LIVING LIGHT. A devotional classic with 732 Scripture selections for morning and evening reading. Kivar and leatherette.

LIVING LIGHT. Giant Print Edition. Scripture selections in giant print for those with limited eyesight.

END OF THE VOLUME.